Handling
Verbal
Confrontation

Other books by Robert V. Gerard, Ph.D.

Lady from Atlantis
> a novel about an Ancient Empress's
> return to Earth and her quest for world
> peace and romanticism

The Corporate Mule
> a real to life comedy drama about a young
> man's ambition within the corporate
> setting, and how he almost loses his soul
> in the quest to achieve the company goal

DNA Healing Techniques
> a practical, "hands on" manual that
> explains the current shift in our DNA, and
> gives step-by-step instructions for activat-
> ing the hitherto dormant DNA in our cells,
> how to conduct a DNA expansion and
> rejuvenation, and how to perform a whole
> body diagnostic reading and healing.

Booklet:

Time: Man's Cosmic Locator
> provides a brief scholarly exposé of the
> philosophical aspects of time as viewed by
> Plato, the Ancient Hebrews, and modern
> day quantum mechanics.

Testimonials

"Gerard has written an accurate and helpful book about how to communicate with people. It is a must for those who want to be effective in the workplace. Read it and make the ideas work for you."

— Dr. Drea Zigarmi

Coauthor of *Leadership and the One Minute Manager*

"Handling Verbal Confrontation is an excellent communication resource that is practical, effective, and invaluable. The Gerard model provides skills and a clear map for negotiation and creative problem-solving during times of conflict. The book is an outstanding classic for peace-making in the 21st Century."

— Angeles Arrien, Cultural Anthropologist

Author of *Four-Fold Way* and *Working Together*

"Are you a gentle soul? Do you walk the other way to avoid confrontation? — or perhaps shake for days if yelled at? If so, *Handling Verbal Confrontation* is for you. It presents a positive win-win situation for communication in these difficult areas. It will inform and uplift... and in the process will give you confidence. The gentle soul remains, but with new empowering tools. It works!"

— Lee Carroll

Author of the Kryon series

"I believe Robert Gerard has made an important contribution to dealing with interpersonal conflict. His direct confrontation empowers all of us to take care of ourselves. The Fix, a clear and repeated request for commitment, is the unique contribution of this book."

— Doug Ross, Ph.D.

Author of *A Tao of Dialogue*

"...this book is indeed an instructional manual for wielding a verbally nonviolent sword in problem-solving dilemmas. ... With plenty of charts, models, examples of confrontation scenarios, and on-the-floor coaching guidelines, this is a hands-on manual for learning how to get along."

— NAPRA ReView

Handling Verbal Confrontation

Take the FEAR Out of Facing Others

Robert V. Gerard, Ph.D.

Published by
OUGHTEN HOUSE FOUNDATION, INC
COARSEGOLD, CALIFORNIA, USA

Handling Verbal Confrontation
Take the FEAR Out of Facing Others
by Robert V. Gerard, Ph.D.

Published by

OUGHTEN HOUSE FOUNDATION, INC.
P.O. Box 1059
COARSEGOLD, CALIFORNIA, 93614 USA

Library of Congress Cataloging-in-Publication Data

Gerard, Robert, 1945-
    Handling verbal confrontations : take the fear out of facing others / Robert Gerard. --
2nd ed.
            p. cm.
    ISBN 1-880666-05-7 : $14.95
    1. Interpersonal confrontation. 2. Interpersonal conflict.
3. Interpersonal communications.   I. Title.
BF637.I48G47 1992
158' .2--dc20   92-24137
                                                    CIP

ISBN 1-880666-05-7, Trade Publication
0 9 8 7 6 5 4 3 2 1

Printed in United States of America
Recycled and acid-free paper used .

Contents

Dedication

For my son Bob who desires to communicate truth,
and to his son, Daniel, my grandson, who only desires to hear the Truth.

*Look your opponent
right in the eyes.
Give him your total attention.*

*Thrust upon him your complete respect.
Cut swiftly through his fears.
He gives you no fight.*

*Your thoughts now shared
demand his creative reply.
Conflict at rest.
Resolution in sight.*

*Find confidence within.
Enjoy your success,
for his growth has been spirited
and his oneness expressed.*

Acknowledgments

I'd like to extend my wholehearted appreciation and gratitude to all the corporate executives, managers, supervisors, teachers, nurses, and parents out there in the work place who experienced growth and contributed to this book. Your participation and feedback was invaluable.

My thanks to Victor R. Beasley, Ph.D., psychologist, anthropologist, and author of *Intuition by Design*, for support and fine work in the field of intuition.

A special "thank you" is extended to all those wonderful students who attended the Confrontation Skills Training Workshops and demonstrated positive changes by using our techniques. It was in the workshops that many of the techniques were put to the test, proven, and refined.

A special acknowledgment goes to my editor, Tony Stubbs. His dedication to turn a very complicated manuscript into a book has to be commended. I knew this well as he began to apply the techniques of this material and truly committed himself to represent the reader in the process of acquiring this material. He created an arrangement of styles used in this book, which enhances comprehension of this large and important body of information. Thank you, Tony!

Above all, let us all give gratitude to God, the *Source* of all information and wisdom.

Foreword

Why do some people appear to sail through life, swiftly and easily overcoming obstacles, while others get bogged down in problems? The answer lies in the ability to confront. Those who face problem situations head on, quickly and decisively, are simply more effective at the game we call "life." Those who recoil from confronting situations and other people are less effective at living. So while you may think that confrontation skills are primarily business skills, they are, in fact, *life skills*, applicable from the boardroom to the bedroom.

There is also a spiritual aspect to confrontation. Our spirit thrives on the human potential for learning and doing. To subdue the spirit through fear is surely a way to misery and loneliness.

Pain instantly occurs when we fail to deal with the issue before us, and to properly confront. We let ourselves down. Sometimes we are abused. But the real tragedy occurs when we deny our spirit a chance to express itself. This must end.

We must move onward, and become masters of our own fate. We must understand the importance of confrontation as a sustaining and fulfilling activity. We must understand that it is our birthright to intuitively explore our world and create relationships in the process.

Hour-by-hour, day-by-day, we continue to mature and develop our mental and spiritual lives. We cultivate our lives ceaselessly: consciously and subconsciously. When we find a moment to stop and ponder, we find ourselves in the midst of accomplishments, which once were our very thoughts. The *Tao Te Ching* expresses this poetically:

> *The softest of stuff in the world*
> *Penetrates quickly the hardest;*
> *Insubstantial, it enters*
> *Where no room is.*

> *By this I know the benefit*
> *Of something done by quiet being;*
> *In all the world but few can know*
> *Accomplishment apart from work,*
> *Instruction when no words are used.*

We must pursue our dreams. We must not falter because we are inhibited by the way we listen and speak *silently* to ourselves or *overtly* to others.

Within this book you will find literally hundreds of ideas, principles, rules, methods, and exercises which build your confidence and improve your ability to confront.

Originally, this book was titled, *The Sword of Confrontation*. Many students who have taken the Confrontation Skills Training Course have asked me how the word "Sword" came about. I adopted it from Bushido philosophy from which the Samurai swordsman cultivated his principles. Our application of the word "Sword" implies the use of knowledge and language. Each word we use during confrontation is like a sword. It cuts through fear, resistance, and self-doubt. Like the symbol of the US Marine Corps, the sword signifies confidence, precision, and the sharpness of our ability to use language.

This book is *not* about combat. It's about learning, improving, and honoring self and others. Like the Samurai swordsman who dedicates and disciplines himself to survive his opponent, we too must discipline and dedicate ourselves to vigorously respond to the challenge of confronting in order to maintain the wellbeing of self, others, and our relationships with them: a "win-win-win" outcome.

Therefore, I do not seek the sharpness of the blade in combat, rather the sharpness of the mind in verbal confrontations. I see a person learning how to properly confront because of his or her dedication to sustained self-improvement. And most importantly, to build upon the relationships in his or her life.

I see change. I see confidence. I see life! And above all, express your spirit and live your heaven.

— *R. V. Gerard*

Introduction

Handling Verbal Confrontation is an uplifting and revealing book which can improve your skill level when verbally confronting others. The book presents a step-by-step method to obtain commitment resulting from win-win-win confrontations. It offers sound advice on how you can build relationships in the midst of adversarial situations. It demonstrates how you can learn to become an accurate communicator and a respected confronter. Also you will have an opportunity to learn how to put an end to fear and make confronting a non-painful event.

Handling Verbal Confrontation is for the general audience. The examples, scenarios, and illustrations used portray business and domestic settings. Depending on the need, the book is intended for managers, parents, teachers, supervisors, nurses, teenagers, bankers, health care providers, realtors, day care workers, police and other social service personnel. Special editions of this work are in preparation that focus on specific occupations and vocations.

Handling Verbal Confrontation presents the Confrontation Model — a proven method which increases your confidence to confront others without fear. In addition to aiding learning and guidance, we also use models to explain the actions illustrated associated with the model's behaviors, styles, and processes.

Two models which will help us achieve higher levels of success when we confront are:

The Accurate Communication Model

and

The Confrontation Model

These models are replicas of some real-world phenomena that we use for increasing insight; just as the hammer and screwdriver are tools for the carpenter, so these models are tools for the architect, the scientist, the manager, and the parent.

The following brief story describes how the Confrontation Model came to be. One day, while I was coaching a supervisor in a manufacturing plant, the supervisor said, "Without a tool, confronting others is too hard for me to do. If I had a some kind of confrontation tool, I could use it to confront my people. You know, something I can see, touch, and feel." He picked up a screw driver and demonstrated his skill using it. Then he turned to me, and said, "Give me a confrontation tool, and I'll develop the skills to use it."

This challenge led me to develop the Confrontation Model. Once it was developed and implemented, it took the form of an interpersonal tool—a paradigm of interaction within human relationships. The managers and supervisors who learned the model's techniques soon realized the benefits of its use.

After applying the model consistently over a brief period of time (also known as behavioral learning), the learners soon used the model out of habit. Once you assimilate the Confrontation Model, you will find yourself using it as if it were one of your everyday tools. Just reach for it, apply it, and you can fix most issues in life with it.

Models permit us to see how things go together. They serve as guidelines which, through *self-coaching,* enable us to get our goals accomplished. Most importantly, we learn from models, hence, we can live out our *confrontation technique* paradigms.

The two models presented in this book have been successfully applied thousands of times. Trust them; give them a chance; learn from them. Grow!

Each model presented is developed slowly, with explanations and examples. The *Communication Model,* covered first, will help us better understand the *Confrontation Model.* You will see that successful confrontation is possible only with accurate communication.

The book presents each model in its basic form, and then develops it step-by-step. When first learning the models, visualize their basics, achieve an orientation to their philosophical precepts, and then get excited about your new tools.

This book builds on a generic Communication Model, making additions where necessary. Plenty of excellent reference material is available for further study of the communication process.

The Confrontation Model is a pyramid, suggesting that climbing it requires effort. It's an upward path which demands that you learn certain "climbing" skills that reflect not only strengths on our part, but also the ability to encourage others to climb. Once we get to the top, you reap the lasting rewards of increased confidence, issue resolution, and personal growth.

Our goal is to resolve the issue by taking it to the top of the pyramid. Keeping focused and staying on your path are key. If we lean away, we could "fall off the pyramid." The confronter and confrontee are on opposite sides of the pyramid, and only through clear and accurate communication can they unite and succeed.

The more we understand and practice with the models, the easier they are to apply. Soon the models become instilled within us as routines. Within a couple of months, our abilities to communicate accurately and confront issues will reach new heights. It is then that we will recognize more successes in life.

Each aspect of the model is carefully explained and grouped within six separate learning diagrams and examples offered. The following topic areas are covered:
- self-confrontation and understanding the need to verbally confront
- identifying the issue
- staying focused and verbally positioned

- properly approaching others in a one-two-three fashion
- accurately stating the facts and maintaining concentration
- rebuttal preparedness and overcoming fear
- prompting change and initiating creative thinking
- standing firm and dealing with defenses
- coaching towards a win-win-win situation
- getting commitment
- self-reward and relationship recognition
- reaching resolution.

Many new techniques of verbal confrontation are provided within each learning diagram. They will guide the reader towards a better understanding and application of a non-hostile approach to resolving conflicts and issues. The psychological importance of the Confrontation Model is meticulously described. The final chapter emphasizes personal growth and spirituality. The reader will be awakened to the realms of thought, self-talk, self-motivation, and basic visualization techniques.

To ease you into the Confrontation Model, it provides three "orientation" stages:

De-scripting — breaking away from our old patterns
Scripting — regenerating new and usable tools
Personalizing — incorporating our new tools into our normal daily behaviors

Each stage accommodates your level of knowledge and comfort within the relationship.

You may think you are already good at confronting issues. Fine! More power to you. But, try to answer the following as honestly as you can:

- Are your confrontation skills based on **aggressive** behavior, whereby your intent is not necessarily an "I win—You win" outcome, but rather a selfish "I win—You lose" outcome?
- Are you a **passive** person who is intimidated by the very thought of confronting others?
- Are you an **assertive** person who just needs the "how to" of successful confrontation?

Which confrontation behavioral type best fits you? Many of us can claim one or two. One of the best ways to find out what type applies to you is to *listen* carefully to your inner voice. Close your eyes for a moment and reflect on your past. Ask yourself this fundamental question:

Can I confront others collaboratively and reach a mutual agreement?

Feel your answer. Verify it. If you can answer *"yes"* to the above questions for the majority of your recent interactions, then this book will reinforce your talents and increase your chances for continued success. If you answer anything other than "yes," then this book is mandatory reading for you. It will allow you to gain the confidence that may substantially improve your life. It will also provide you with the basic confrontation tools you need to perform your job effectively.

Handling Verbal Confrontation contains *proven* methods that improve your people skills to handle problems. Regardless of where you work, you've probably heard these statements over a thousand times:

"He's so difficult to deal with. How do I handle him?"

"What we need around here is better communication!"

"This place needs to get its act together!"

"I wish I could do something about it."

Well, you can! You dream and hope that someday other people will hear and listen to you. To gain the confidence that demands attention and respect, **you** must first develop the knowledge and tools required for productive confrontation. It will take you a few weeks, lots of practice, maybe a friend to help you, and some planning.

One of the best things about learning these methods is that you become more *confident*. You can look a person straight in the eye without fear, exchange concise and meaningful information, earn respect, and drive the interaction to a mutually beneficial conclusion.

Handling Verbal Confrontation was written to provide you with a *verbal* tool. Once you adequately learn to use it, you will enjoy profound changes, such as improved confidence, diminished fear, and more improved peace of mind.

Above all, when we use this tool properly, our lives become clearer as we deal with the reality around us. Be your own witness and realize then how much more freedom you have to enjoy!

Verbal Confrontation —
The Forgotten Art!

*"The process of confronting teaches us
how to better understand ourselves, which in turn,
enables us to confront others with more success."*

— *Robert Gerard*

One of the major inadequacies of our culture is our inability to verbally confront one another. It kills interpersonal relationships. It is a time bomb within families. It causes low productivity, promotes mediocre performance, business failures, law suits, marital arguments, boredom, and apathy. It creates stress and heartaches. It increases our consumption of aspirin, alcohol, and drugs. Very few even recognize it as a problem, and even fewer know what to do about it.

The Forgotten Art!

Did your school ever teach you how to confront verbally? Was confronting others part of your English or Speech class? A few of us have been trained in these areas, most notably, lawyers, military personnel, executives, and sales people. But what about employees of a large organization? You?

When an issue or situation is not properly confronted, can you sense the frustration? Can you feel the tension of the situation increase? The turmoil and confusion? Do you know the cost of the loss of trust, confidence, and money? The *forgotten art* of saying what's on your mind from the bottom of your heart has gone to pasture. Our ability to stand for our rights has been replaced by apathy, superficiality, and "anything for a quiet life."

Well, my friends, those days are about to end. You are about to learn a new and proven technique that will help you to confront verbally and reach a mutual agreement through collaboration.

At the heart of conflict resolution lies the more sophisticated process of **confrontation**. Confronting simply means *addressing* or *attending to* an **issue**—not aggressive combat! Later, we will develop a detailed model of confrontation, but for the moment, let's clarify four important terms:

- **Issue** — the essential point of, and reason for, the discussion which needs to be confronted and mutually resolved.

- **Confronting** — the verbal, face-to-face process of dealing with the issue; it also connotes dealing with one's inward self (self-confrontation).
- **Intent** — the prevailing motive that necessitates the need to resolve the issue that has brought unbalance to the relationship. The intents of the parties within the relationship may coincide or conflict, and they may or may not be revealed to the other party.
- **Outcome** — the situation that will prevail when the issue has been resolved. We call this "Win–Win–Win" because both parties, *and* the relationship all benefit.

The element of *issue* is crucial. It is the focus of the exchange within the confrontation process. During the dialogue, if we get off on tangents, fail to listen attentively, prejudge, or become inhibited, then we lose focus on the *issue*. Once that happens, confusion and mixed signals set in, resulting in more problems and the need for another round of confrontation. If this also fails, the original issue can escalate in width and depth, eventually getting out of control and consuming both parties.

Why Confront?

Learning to confront inevitably leads to better understanding yourself as a person. Your ability to properly develop your ego depends partially on your ability to confront yourself *inwardly*. The more success we have when confronting personal situations (doubt, fears, prejudice, etc.), the less suppression occurs and the greater the desire and opportunity to create personal satisfaction.

The greater the ability to confront difficult people, the less suppression and self-doubt occurs. Instead, things get done! You become more confident and resonate with self-motivation. Opportunities for increased personal and social satisfaction appear.

In a sense, handling conflict and fear raises consciousness, and successful resolution promotes well-being. Here's why. Up to this point in time, you may have had many unresolved issues or fears in your life—some big, some small, and some related to other issues. It has been proven that unresolved issues become psychologically embedded in the human body.

The term "dis-ease" originates from this concept—the body is not "at ease." As each unresolved embedded issue or fear resides within you, some that are similar or related attach themselves to each other, making larger embedded structures! For some people, these become phobias. Such people can have hundreds of embedded structures within them. But fortunately, most of us have a manageable number, and relief is on the way. As you will soon learn, self-confronting eliminates these embedded structures, and confronting current and approaching issues and fears prevents further buildup of potential obstacles in your life.

On reading this book, and if possible, completing the confrontation course available, you will have developed self-confrontation and confronting skills. As you live your life each day, you will begin to self-confront embedded structures as well as face any new issues and fears. This is your "cleaning out period," so to speak.

Once you demonstrate confidence and consistency in handling verbal confrontation, you will notice how easily you prevent future issues and fears from manifesting within you. You become "lighter," less burdened, and will demonstrate a new sense of freedom.

Why we need to confront is basic to survival and spiritual growth. The less "disease," that is, garbage we have inside, the lighter and more resilient we are to live creatively, peacefully, and freely as loving beings.

Accurate Communication

Proper confrontation is largely dependent on good communication skills. Our ability to speak effectively, listen carefully, and maintain an interactive dialogue is essential. It is without question that speaking and listening effectively enhances the outcome of most conversations. Within the many models of effective communication, an new term, accurate communication, has emerged.

Accurate Communication emphasizes *clarity* and *intent* within the delivery of the communication process, is results- and relationship-oriented, and promotes behavioral change, and most important, is a "whole being" process. Chapter 4 presents more information on Accurate Communication.

Among the benefits of *Accurate Communication* are that it:
- Sets the stage for your total performance
- Encourages you to define your intent
- Increases your intuition
- Creates a better understanding
- Enhances your expression
- Provokes behavior change
- Achieves completion of intent
- Reduces stress levels
- Facilitates speaking from the "heart."

Why Listen?

Listening is an integral part of communicating. In fact, more than half the time you spend during communicating is spent listening, so let's look at the importance listening plays when confronting.

Many problems at home and work occur because we don't bother to listen. If you think that you have the ability to listen perfectly, then maybe you are perfect. But if you find yourself toiling over what other people say, then the need for improving your listening skills exists; and ... you're not perfect.

There are *two kinds* of listening. Which of them do you think is more important?

> Listening to others, or
>
> Listening to yourself

The second is more important because we can *only* listen to others once we can listen attentively to ourselves.

Please give this next statement some thought:

"You cannot confront others until you can confront yourself."

Many people lack the skills to properly confront others, so they withdraw and fail to properly confront the issue. Compounding the problem, if you attempt to confront and fail, your confidence weakens, thus undermining future confrontations. Also, many cultures (e.g., Chinese, Japanese, Arabian) consider confrontation, especially with elders, to be disrespectful, or even insulting. However, most English speaking cultures will greatly benefit from improved confrontation skills.

Listen more closely to your own thoughts, feelings and actions when you want to confront another. Listening to yourself and confronting yourself are the first steps toward successful confrontation and handling difficult people. A few questions may prove revealing:

- Do you handle yourself well in front of other people?
- Are you often asked to contribute input or state your opinion?
- Can you speak effectively and get your point across?
- Do you handle difficult people well?

We must listen to ourselves and find out our real needs. If you answered "no" to any one of these questions, then take a serious look inside. We must take inventory of our confrontation abilities. Let's truthfully acknowledge the fact that we must change before we expect others to change.

Confronting and Listening are Interdependent

The best communicators in the home and workplace are, for the most part, the best listeners. Good listeners detect the most important elements of a conversation. They seek facts and understand the reasoning of others.

Rule #1:   *When you truly understand what others are saying, then and only then, can you correctly respond.*

When good communication doesn't occur, a breakdown results. Not to understand the message is like running a red light. Worse yet, to assume that you understand when you don't is like running a red light in front of a police car. You *will* pay the price for it!

Reading and working through this book can be fun. You will have the opportunity to learn two very essential aspects of life:

- Confronting yourself
- Confronting others

The payoff is that you will become an accurate communicator, experience personal growth, and be joyfully rewarded. You will begin to experience new levels of personal creativity, and personal doubts and inhibitions will disappear. As you confront issues, you will gain confidence. You will carry less baggage and become more free!

After only a few weeks of putting the Confrontation Model to practice, you will find yourself confronting yourself more often. You will confront and resolve trivial matters consciously and unconsciously. A major benefit of this to you is *having more time*. Less trivia, less doubt, less hassling events means more time for you to *be yourself!*

Samples of Poor Confrontation

Millions of examples of poor confrontation occur daily simply because people cannot properly confront what they need to in order to get a desired result. For example, while flying to Minneapolis-St. Paul, I witnessed an airline stewardess trainee receiving terrible instructions on serving in-flight dinners. The senior stewardess with a tray in her hands pointed up and down to several aisles. She repeated herself inconsistently as her face expressed annoyance. The trainee looked completely confused and kept saying: "But ..." while nodding her head up and down in agreement.

Suddenly, the conversation stopped. The new recruit grabbed hold of the aisle food cart, exhaled a harsh breath upwards into her falling hair, rolled her eyes in turmoil, and pushed the cart past me. Was this a well thought out training experience?

What happened? First, the senior stewardess failed to confront herself. She needed to face the fact ("address an issue") that she wasn't making sense with the instructions she was giving the trainee. Secondly, the trainee got upset and confused, and failed to confront the manner and inconsistency of the instructions given by the senior stewardess. There is more to investigate, but this was more than a communication problem — it was a *confrontation problem.*

Rule #2:   ***Underlying almost every confrontation problem is a communication problem.***

Orientations

There are three orientations within the confrontation process:

1. Confronting oneself (self-confrontation)
2. Confronting another person, issue, thing or event
3. Confronting difficult people

The most critical is *self-confrontation.* Unless you can confront your own hidden agendas and deal with yourself, how can you expect to face others? The most challenging is handling difficult people because part of their counter-attack is to upset your confidence and ability to confront them. We will have more to say about these so called "negatives" later.

To productively resolve the problem, good confrontation skills are required. Each example in this chapter presents an obvious communication problem as well as a hidden confrontation problem for discussion.

Familiar Scenarios

Examples within this book are real life situations—at home, on the job and otherwise. Many of these scenarios relate to parent-child, and manager-supervisor. They offer us an analysis and potential solutions, as well. The Appendix contains a variety of the self-paced learning exercises.

Scenario: In the CEO's office

Who's Involved: CEO and Jones, the Director of Human Resources

The CEO, Mr. McKenzie, summons the Director of Human Resources, Mr. Bob Jones to his office. Mr. Jones, who has been with the company for twelve years, demonstrates a typical reactive management mood. [The key word here is "reactive."]

"Yes, sir, Mr. McKenzie! What can I do for you?"

McKenzie's eyebrows rise, "Plenty!"

Jones interprets this as a good opportunity and prepares to receive an important assignment.

"Bob, we've got to get our people to be more productive on the third shift."

"Yes, you're right, sir."

"What do you think we ought to do, Bob?"

"Well, we can call in the Training Department."

"Nah! That takes too long," McKenzie says critically.

Afraid to say something wrong, Jones merely stares. The chief exec turns away from his director, walks a few steps towards his extravagant mahogany desk, and commands, "We just have to get tough with those supervisors down there."

"Yes, sir!"

"Good!" says McKenzie. "Let me know how we stand with this by our next monthly meeting."

"Will do, Mr. McKenzie."

Jones leaves the office suite. He wonders: Will do what? What have I committed to this time? By the next meeting; that's nineteen days from now. Oh shit!

The events in the situation are condensed, of course; but the point is clear—this everyday top-down dialogue is the cause of many problems. The CEO wanted results. How? He really didn't know. Jones, unprepared and reactive, committed himself to a task which he did not truly understand. Will Bob Jones get productivity up on the third shift? Or, has he fallen into the *poor confrontations pit*? How will he get out of this one?

Let's analyze the above dialogue:

- Did either party communicate any accurate understanding?
- What was the real assignment?
- Was an expected outcome communicated? If so, was it quantified?
- Did Bob Jones attempt to find out the facts?
- Did Jones get a true understanding of McKenzie's awareness of the realities on the third shift?
- Did Jones get support and commitment from McKenzie?
- Did McKenzie get commitment from Jones?
- Will McKenzie and Jones succeed in their efforts to improve productivity on the third shift. Or, will they serve as catalysts for creating more problems?

As we mentioned in Chapter 1, within the process of conflict resolution, the more sophisticated process of confrontation occurs. Confronting—*addressing an issue*—simply means *getting to the point and resolving an issue.*

The *issue* is the focus of the confrontation exchange. During the dialogue, if we get off on tangents, fail to listen attentively to the message, prejudge, or become inhibited, then we are no longer focused on the *issue*. Once that happens, confusion and mixed signals set in and we may create more problems.

In addition to the communication problems we analyzed in the above scenario, a number of *poor confrontations* also occurred. Let's replay it with a few comments to guide you *[within brackets]*:

"Yes sir, Mr. McKenzie! What can I do for you?" [Bob prejudges the intent of the meeting]

McKenzie's eyebrows rise, "Plenty!" [Bob gets emotional]

"Bob, we've got to get our people to be more productive on the third shift." [vague]

"Yes, you're right sir." [reactive]

"What do you think we ought to do, Bob?"

[What is the issue? *Bob needs to confront the CEO. "What are your real concerns about the third shift, Mr. McKenzie?"]*

"Well, we can call in the Training Department." [quick fix mentality]

[Bob *did not probe the CEO for specifics, facts, or intent.*]

"Nah! That takes too long," says McKenzie, critically.

[McKenzie compounds the exchange of information by permitting Jones to take a passive stance, when instead, Jones should have offered a few recommendations.]

"We just have to get tough with those supervisors down there." [compounding confusion]

[Now Jones is challenged, but on what issue?]

"Yes sir!"

[Jones commits himself to solve the unspecified problem.]

"Good!" says McKenzie. "Let me know how we stand with this by our next monthly meeting." [reciprocal commitment]

[Jones commits to furnish information without knowing the CEO's real issue.]

"Will do, Mr. McKenzie."

Summarizing, Jones could have found the basis of the CEO's concern through probing or confronting the real issues at hand. Perhaps the CEO didn't know the answer and called Jones in to get more insight. However, Jones reacted and displayed inhibitions. He caved in, and lead McKenzie to believe that he would solve the problem of productivity on the third shift. The issue was never properly identified, agreed upon, or thought through. Needless to say, a severe problem occurred: both Jones and McKenzie misunderstood each other, and the integrity of their relationship weakened.

An improved scenario would be:

"Mr. McKenzie!"

Jones listens attentively.

"Bob," says McKenzie, "we've got to get our people to be more productive on the third shift."

"Sir, do the facts suggest the cause of low productivity is people or operations?

"Productivity is low. That's all I have. It's lower than I want it to be. What do you think we ought to do, Bob?"

"I'll need to get more facts and assess the situation."

"Get back with me by the end of next week," said McKenzie.

"I'll give you a pre-assessment. We'll get a hold on the problem, Mr. McKenzie."

"Good!"

In this case, Jones didn't permit himself to become part of the problem. Instead, he kept objective and sought the facts. That kind of confrontation skill earns respect, especially from a superior like McKenzie.

Rule #3: **_The best preventive medicine for problems is accurate communication—confronting the issue at hand._**

Our next confrontation sample takes us to a familiar situation which most of us have experienced many times.

> **Scenario:** **The Deadly Hallway Assignment**
> **Who's Involved: Supervisor to Employee**

You work in the accounting office of a manufacturing plant. You have just come out of the rest room and are returning to your desk. Approaching you in the hallway is your supervisor. You look at him. Your thoughts (Self-Talk) search for a simple greeting (senseless trivia) in preparation for quick conversation. Unfortunately, your supervisor is upset. Then it happens — the quick _hallway trash_:

> Boss: "I could have guessed I'd find you here."
> You: Silently you mumble: "You poor soul, never a positive word." However, you manage to crack a smile.
> Boss: "Will you please check the balance of the Tri-Kon account."
> You: "Yes, sir!"

The fleeting exchange is over. Your boss has passed by you, and your brief visit to the rest room has afforded you more discomfort. Your mental frame of _reference_ is rapidly deteriorating into fear. You were not prepared to meet the boss, nor were you mentally alert enough to understand his assignment. Most importantly, you were not skillful enough to get an accurate assessment (or a _true understanding_) of the assignment. "Good grief, Charlie Brown!" Another example of poor communications once again has taken its toll.

The ball is now in your court. You need some answers to a few basic questions:

- Why do I need to check the Tri-Kon account?
- When do I need to do it?
- How important is it?
- What information do I need to support my findings?

The _true understanding_ of the assignment was not conveyed. The only thing that occurred was a troublesome and unfriendly hallway encounter. Nothing was accomplished, except the deterioration of a relationship; and a personal problem was reinforced. The scenario depicts a poorly communicated work assignment. It reflects the tragedy that the assignment did not reveal motive or create enthusiasm. This reduced any sense of creativity and provoked discontent. Communicating in this manner made for ineffective work, and reduced collaboration because you don't know why you're doing what you're doing.

Let's replay the above scenario and analyze how it lacked any sense of a _confrontation_.

Boss: "I could have guessed I'd find you here." [The supervisor was sarcastic and demeaning. Instead, he could have introduced an issue or concern about the Tri-Kon account.]

You: Silently you mumble: You poor soul, never a positive word. However, you manage to crack a smile.
[Instead of your defensive and judgmental response, you could have challenged the supervisor with: "Good guess. What can I do for you?" (Probing for the issue.) At this point, the issue and work assignment could have been revealed, preventing deterioration of the relationship and introduction of other poor work habits.]

Boss: "Will you please check the balance of the Tri-Kon account." [states the importance and creates the intent]

You: "Yes sir!" [premature commitment without knowing the purpose]

Now, let's polish it up:

Boss: "I could have guessed I'd find you here."
You: "Thanks!"
Boss: "Will you please check the balance of the Tri-Kon account."
You: "Are there any specifics I need to know?"
Boss: "Yes. I need to know when we received their last payment. And I need to have that information before 4 o'clock, today."
You: "I'll get that information to you."

Do you see how good confrontation skills play an important role in work efficiency and interpersonal relationships? Now, let's move on and look at a marital situation to demonstrate a point about agreement.

Scenario: Poor Marital Communications
Who's Involved: Husband and Wife

Husband: "Do you want to go out for dinner tonight?"
Wife: "Well, what do you feel like eating?"
Husband: "Anything that pleases you."
Wife: "I really don't care; it doesn't matter to me."
Husband: "Why do you always throw it back at me?"
Wife: "I don't always do that! You're too damned sensitive."
Husband: "That's not true. You just can't ever make a decision."
Wife: "You can leave that corporate crap at work!"
Husband: "Well, the hell with you! I'll make a bologna sandwich."
Wife: "You didn't really want to go out to dinner anyway."

This scenario can go anywhere our imagination wants to take it. The critical question was: *Where was accurate (true) understanding conveyed?*

Let's look at an alternative to that scenario where *true understandings* and feelings for each other are properly expressed.

Husband:	"I feel like going out to dinner tonight, How about you?"
Wife:	"Sure. What do you feel like eating?"
Husband:	"Maybe Chinese or Italian."
Wife:	"Mexican!"
Husband:	"Nah!"
Wife:	"Mexican!"
Husband:	"You're persuasive; and I love you for it."

In this scenario, the couple communicated true understandings. They acted in a creative and positive frame of reference. The rest came naturally. For this chapter, our final example depicts a scene between a mother and teenage daughter.

Scenario: Doing household chores
Who's Involved: Mother, Ann, and her daughter, Aubree

Mother:	"Hi, Aubree. Listen, I need to speak to you."
Daughter:	"What's up, mom?"
Mother:	"The chores."
Daughter:	"Oh, yeah … the chores."
Mother:	"What's the plan."
Daughter:	"I guess I should do them right away."
Mother:	"That sounds good to me."
Daughter:	"It won't take too long, anyway."
Mother:	"I'll get a snack ready for us. Okay?"
Daughter:	"Great!"

Sounds simple? With the right techniques, the above scenario is very probable. The word "you" was never mentioned in challenge. The mother stayed objective, said very few words, and committed to a reward. Aubree had very little distraction. She was guided to use her own positive thoughts to resolve the issue — the chores. Nothing else entered the confrontation dialogue to distract from, instead of focus on, the issue.

Rule #4:   *Express what you feel – expressing what you feel is your only obligation. Be truthful about it! That's the breath of ·life. There's no hidden intention, motive or agenda. It's a feeling of freedom, it instills confidence. It earns respect. It's fun. It really is!*

How Do Confrontation Skills Benefit Me?

Do peace of mind and more confidence sound good? Want more? In this chapter, we itemize many benefits for the parent, teacher, the teenager, the professional, the working manager and the line supervisor.

When we communicate and *confront* more accurately, we, in essence, rid ourselves of misdirections and assumptions. Facts and information surface readily with clear conversation. Reasons for problems such as low productivity no longer hide in reports or someone's head—they are known! Interpersonal relationships begin to improve because issues and inconsistencies are confronted and resolved.

Reasons not to remedy problems are reduced simply because solutions may have already been communicated. When problem resolution occurs, everyone is more open and receptive, which leads to accountability and creativity. In the workplace, interactions become more concise, confident, and less costly.

What do we mean by "less costly?" Simply that the less time spent talking (beating around the bush), the more time is availabale for action and performance. The following scenario proves the point about the meaning of "less costly."

Scenario: Standing next to a desk-top computer
Who's involved: Marketing supervisor, Bob and specialist, Jan.

Bob: "When will the new marketing demo be ready, Jan?"
Jan: "That depends on Frank's input for the menu."
Bob: "What menu are you talking about?"
Jan: "Selection of Client Characteristics."
Bob: "Oh!"
Jan: "Well, anyway, Frank told me he'd have what I need by two o'clock. It doesn't matter."
Bob: "What doesn't matter?"
Jan: "Don't worry, Bob. Frank will give me what I need."
Bob: "Jan, all I need to know is when the marketing demo will be ready!"
Jan: "Ah, about five today."
Bob: "Thanks!"

In order to figure out how much the above conversation cost, we need to compare it to something in order to get a variance (a difference between two events). Therefore, let's create an improved version of the above conversation:

> Bob: "Jan, when will the new marketing demo be ready?
> Jan: "About five today."
> Bob: "Thanks!"

The first conversation took 45 seconds. The second version took only 5 seconds and saved 40 seconds of lost-time. If you have ten of these interactions a day, these savings add up to 40 hours a year—an extra week! And that doesn't even begin to count the benefits of higher productivity.

Accurate communication is vitally important. Overall, it helps improve organizational effectiveness; people know what's going on in the workplace and have a better understanding of the concerns and issues involving their jobs. Now imagine how much savings a company could acquire if proper verbal confrontation techniques were used.

Improved *verbal confrontations* can benefit you. Check off which of the following benefits you would like to enjoy:

For the executive:

- Increase productivity
- Develop a more competent staff
- Improve top-down and bottom-up information flow
- Demonstrate better control of resources (material, labor, inventory)
- Improve problem-solving
- Obtain quicker results
- Instill accurate reporting
- Show more flexibility to accommodate change
- Transform from a reactive to a more creative staff
- Increase *no-nonsense* communications
- Save thousands of dollars annually

For managers, supervisors and employees improved communication and confrontation skills help:

- Establish long-term behavioral change
- Transfer problem-solving responsibilities directly to those who are accountable
- Reduce stress in the confronter
- Develop confidence in the confronter (manager, supervisor)
- Establish respect
- Complete the communication process thoroughly
- Help eliminate recurring problems
- Reduce lost-time
- Supervisor doesn't have to go back repeatedly to the same worker
- Supervisor is more concise and swift
- Employees will act in accordance with the supervisor's behavior
- Avoid trivia and reduce excessive socializing

- Eliminate emotional defenses
- Provoke thinking on the part of the confrontee (accountability)
- Encourage employees to be more responsible
- Use facts to solve problems
- Seek a win/win/win outcome
- Detect lying
- Serve to identify other related issues
- Demand attention and accuracy
- Define expectations clearly
- Provide personal growth and feedback
- Increase the quickness of problem-solving
- Encourage teamwork among the supervisors
- Spark the individual pursuit of excellence
- Enable the supervisor to further develop his or her concentration
- Initiate excitement and self-motivation
- Identify strong and competent supervisors
- Identify those who seek change
- Help the human resources succession planning function
- Build character

For the parent:

- Reduce tension within the home
- Improve conversations with your spouse and children
- Close the gap between old and new by resolving problems as they occur
- Increase spontaneity in your daily conversations
- Be more precise and understood when addressing your children
- Enjoy earning more respect
- Show concern and understanding when communicating with children
- Show more willingness to accommodate verbal interaction
- Reduce negative reactive to a more creative environment
- Get your point across
- Demonstrate that you care and have feelings, too

For the teenager:

- Improve your confidence to speak your word
- Enhance self-esteem and to advocate your concerns and beliefs
- Express your feelings
- Ask for clarity
- Present your position or situation with clarity
- Speak maturely to adults
- Clarify issues and negate peer pressure
- Protect yourself against negative peer associations
- Defend what's important to you
- Feel better and comfortable about who you are and where you are

- Seek friendship and enhance the opportunity to improve relationships
- Reduce internal fears by seeking the truth and finding what's right for you
- Feel more in control when on dates or among friends

How many did you check? Only you know what's best for yourself, your employees, and your family. Reading and practicing the techniques in this book, and eventually taking the *Confrontation Skills Training Workshop* will satisfy the needs you identified above.

Interpersonal Communication

In this chapter, we will enhance our understanding of communication. We will revitalize the importance of communication, debunk some of the myths surrounding it, and explore some new dynamics. The emphasis is on "whole being" or "total person" communication.

Once we have a firm foundation of Interpersonal Communication, we can transport our new skills over to the Confrontation Model. We'll continue to learn new dimensions, psychological and behavioral, which when tactfully applied, will forever change our way of confronting others as well as ourselves.

Interpersonal Communications Redefined

Effective communication can be defined as "the effective transfer of information between two entities (people, governments, computers, etc.) so that understanding is conveyed." But effective communication is just part of the story. Just as important as clarity is the integrity of the communication—that is, what you say is what you feel at the deepest levels of your being. This is Accurate Communication—honest, in alignment with your whole being, and free of the confusing verbal games that most of us play. Many people, therefore, do not thoroughly grasp the essence of what *Interpersonal Communication* entails, and we will slowly develop that process in this book. But first, we need to attain a good grasp of what communication is and how it serves you.

Handling Verbal Confrontations focuses primarily on interaction and that usually means two-way communication—between at least two people—or *interpersonal* communication. Explore your thoughts on this process: take a couple of moments, think deeply, and jot down on a piece of paper your best definition of the term *interpersonal communication*.

When you believe that you have developed a good definition, ask yourself whether you could sell it to your boss, your spouse, or a friend? If you have any doubts, let's examine our definition of interpersonal communications.

Interpersonal communication is a two-way process of conveying a True Understanding between at least two people. It is accomplished in a precise, clear, and forthright manner. A True Understanding occurs when the sender and the receiver fully comprehend what has been communicated—verbally and nonverbally, and what has been communicated can be acknowledged convincingly.

True Understanding

The key ingredient in the communication process is *True Understanding*. And that simply means: was the message properly understood by the recipient?

Most people do not work hard at listening to what others are saying. It has also been proven that people HEAR what they want to hear, which is a form of denial. Major conflicts and confrontations occur because what is being heard and interpreted is not necessarily what is being *said*.

Unless the speaker has a very good hold on the communication process, chances are high that the message being communicated is not thoroughly understood—poor quality control!

For our purposes, we need to ascertain that a *True Understanding* of what was being communicated was received, interpreted, and acknowledged.

When I say, "I enjoy the children bouncing the red ball," what is my intent, and what *True Understanding* do I want on the part of the listener? Do I enjoy (1) "children," 2) "children playing," or 3) "the red, bouncing ball"? The message and intent is not specifically clear. Then how can the listener arrive at a proper *True Understanding* of my intent?

Therefore, the basis of *True Understanding* begins with the speaker, who ideally phrases the *intent* so that it can be understood! This process reduces the liability of poor interpretation. The more focused and clearer the original communication, the less the chance for faulty interpretation and error in the dialogue.

As we shall see later in this chapter, obtaining "acknowledgment" of the *True Understanding* by the listener is the responsibility of the speaker.

Communication is not simply saying something with the hope that what was said was understood and that the right response will occur. Remember:

True Understanding is the sharpness of thought!
True Understanding is the openness of heart!
True Understanding cuts the bull!
True Understanding generates the results!

Two-way Communication

Two-way communication implies that at least two people are in some kind of dialogue. Because you can't be absolutely sure that the other party fully understands your meaning, you look for eye contact, body movements, and other non-verbal communication.

"Listen carefully because what I am going to talk about concerns making a lot of money."

Figure 4.1 graphically shows the communication process for the statement above:

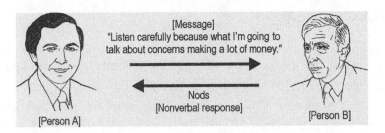

Figure 4.1 - Two-way communication

Did you, as person B, the listener, understand that message? Did you feel energized by it? Did you agree with the statement (that is, mentally saying "Yes"), even though, you did not yet know what that something is? If you answered "yes" to yourself for each question, then we communicated a *True Understanding*. If you were not sure of your response, *True Understanding* was not established.

Assume for a moment that when you communicate to another person, you are 100% accurate in what you say. That is, you are the model of clarity. If the other person gives you only 50% of his or her attention, we multiply these figures to come up with 50% for the actual communication process. If the other party simply isn't listening, he or she is contributing 0%, so the accuracy is 0%. If your transmission is only 50% accurate, and the receiver is only 50% tuned in, the accuracy is 25%.

Suppose you consistently communicate with 90% precision, but your friend is not a good communicator and has a rating of 50%. That equates to 90% x 50%, or 45% communication precision—pretty scary. You would probably be dissatisfied with that level of accuracy and would insist that communicating *True Understanding* between you be improved.

We now explore the Interpersonal Communication Model, Figure 4-2 below.

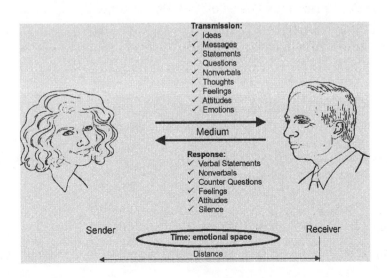

Step-by-step explanation

Speaker: The person who sends or generates the communications. Suppose you want to ask your friend a question. The moment you begin speaking, or even making a nonverbal gesture, you become the sender.

Listener: The person who receives and interprets the message. This could be your friend, who becomes aware of your approach or intent to speak.

Transmission: The communications sent by the *sender*. These take their form in words, bodily gestures, eye contact (happy/sad face, smiles, stance, etc.). This is what the recei*ver* hears and sees.

Response: The new communication generated by the receiver. This is also called an acknowledgment. This is what the receiver says back to you: verbally or nonverbally.

Medium: The vehicle which delivers the communication to the receiver (verbal, nonverbal, written, video, memos). Consider also, the manner and atmosphere surrounding the method of communication: emotions, fear, trust, noise, the environment.

Distance: How physically apart the sender and receiver are. Two other aspects of distance are psychological distance (intelligence and cognition) and level of mutual understanding (common goals and purpose).

Timing: *Emotional space.* Think of time and space as a big invisible cell, and located within are the sender and receiver. Within that cell, the *span of attention* and the *value of how much time* needs to be dedicated to the communication are subconsciously calculated. It's like an invisible clock ticking away. The sender and receiver both evaluate time occurring in the emotional space. If *True Understanding* does not occur *swiftly*, within the emotional space, then an alarm will set off. The alarm can be triggered by the sender or receiver.

Example: Suppose the Sender has something important to say and the Receiver hesitates or somehow signals non-responsiveness. An alarm sounds off in the Sender—emotional space is collapsing.

So, in a Two-Way Communication cycle, the sender is face-to-face (depending on the application of media and method such as a phone) with the receiver. Verbally and nonverbally, a communication is transmitted by the sender. The receiver interprets the communication and responds with a new communication to the sender—nothing more ... nothing less.

Core Elements of the Interpersonal Communication Model

On the next page, Figure 4.3 presents the core elements of the Communication Model.

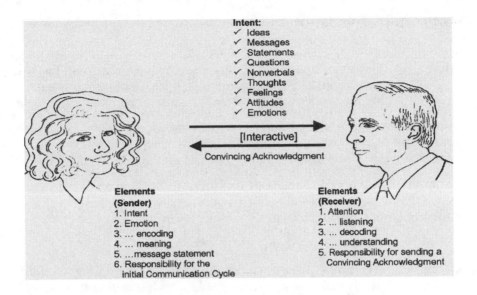

Figure 4-3 Step-by-step Explanation (Speaker)

Intent: The purpose and goal of the communication. The sender must con-
            sciously determine the *intent* to communicate something to the re-
            ceiver. Think of *intent* as the *topic* that is on your mind. It is the mind's
            energizing force to create or change something.

We basically communicate in order to satisfy our intent. The reasoning or objective of whatever resides in our thoughts is directed toward the receiver. We do this
by invoking communication to get the receiver to respond to our wants, our needs,
and a desired win-win-win outcome.

Example (A): You need to tell your manager about his lack of feedback to you.
The *intent* is not his lack of feedback, but rather, it is *your need* to have proper feedback to exist on the job. If you stressed his deficiency, it could come back to haunt
you. If you stressed your need, he may be less threatened and more apt to respond
positively.

Example (B): Your snoring keeps your spouse or significant other awake. If he or
she asks if you're sleeping well, the intent is about your welfare. Instead, he or she
could have said, "Your snoring bothers me!" The intent here reflects his or her discomfort without any concern for you.

Example (C): Suppose your supervisor says, "You don't work fast enough." Is the
intent to get you to work faster?" Or is the intent to increase company profits? Or to
avoid complaints from upper management? If the words: "You don't work fast enough,"
do not truly reflect the supervisor's intent, then another interpersonal problem has

just been created. You may be misled and may soon find out that your boss does not have your best interests in mind. If this happens often, trust is eventually destroyed.

Emotion: The surge of energy, the impulse, or force that puts the "intention" into action. It's the feeling of *need*. It makes the *intent* possible by giving the sender the excitement or cause to communicate the "intent."

Example (A): If your "intent" is to have your employee, Marlene, congratulate you on your recent promotion (an acknowledgment), your emotion is: I *really* want to tell Marlene about my promotion. Note the emphasis on the need, "really."

Example (B): You need to tell your son to lower the volume of his stereo. When you say, "The music is very loud," your emotion is discomfort. You don't necessarily have to shout, but a simple facial gesture may convey nonverbal emotion.

Encoding: The mental process of putting together your thoughts and forming words into logical arrangements. This fascinating process of linguistics requires extensive reading and is beyond the scope of our book. Additional reading is recommended.

Meaning: After having formed your thoughts, will they make sense to the receiver? Can the receiver follow and understand what you have to say? Consider his or her manner of communicating. Some people can take jokes, some cannot. Some request direct and candid statements, others prefer less formal dialogue.

Message Statement: This is the actual verbal or nonverbal communication. Whatever resided in your mind has just left your mouth or expressed by your body. It's out, and the receiver's interpretation begins.

Example: "Marlene, I've got great news to tell you!"

RULE #5:   **The success of the initial communication is solely the responsibility of the sender.**

The principle that the *sender is responsible for the initial communication* is very important! The fulfillment of the *intent* must be achieved. Once the sender is motivated to communicate something, the same motivation also seeks to obtain a response aligned to the purpose of the message. Remember, never permit yourself to get distracted or influenced by other topics or conversation until you receive the proper response. Your INTENT requires satisfaction.

RULE #6:   **During the initial communication, the sender must demand full attention from the receiver. If not, then the receiver is not fully attentive. Do not proceed — stop! Repeat from the beginning if appropriate.**

If you don't have the receiver's undivided attention, you're wasting your time. Should full attention not be ascertained, then the rest of the dialogue may very well be burdened with errors or misunderstandings.

Example: Recall the example about your son's loud music. If he said: "Mom...it's sounds great loud. You just don't appreciate music." Suppose you bought his thought "... you (mom) don't appreciate music," then you've lost control and responsibility for the initial communication. The music is discomforting to you (mom), that's your *intent* and now witness your *emotion* defend your position by your increase in adrenaline.

In summary, each of the **elements** for the sender, stated above, are essential for proper communications. The two most critical elements are *intent* and *responsibility* for the communication. Both play an extremely important role in the Confrontation Model, also. Intent brings purpose into the conversation, while responsibility brings in determination to obtain *True Understanding*.

Step-by-step explanation (Listener/Receiver):

Attention: The Receiver's primary obligation is to give the Sender full attention. To ensure a *True Understanding*, the more the Receiver attends to the communication, the greater the opportunity to comprehend the "Intent" of the Sender.

Example: Suppose you're walking in the park with a friend. She says, "You know, I could go for a salad and a cup of tea." You, on the other hand, are daydreaming about sailing on the open sea.

She says, "Well, what about you?"

You reply, "Sure, I'd love to go sailing."

"What?"

Listen: Do not prejudge or prematurely conclude what the sender's message is saying. Listening to each word the sender says and visualizing them is important. Try not to put your own words in what the sender is saying. Listen! Listen! Listen! If you put your own words in his message, then you're listening to yourself. That's a big mistake! It is critically important for you to respect what the other is saying to you.

Decoding: The mental process of taking apart the message and putting it into your logical frame of reference. As each word enters your mind, be sure you know its definition. This is the other side of encoding.

Example: In the sentence, "The new manager subjugated the experienced supervisor," if you don't know the meaning of the word "subjugated," you could make a serious decoding error.

Understanding: The process by which the Receiver ties together all the words and derives a meaning from the message. Also, understanding assimilates nonverbal messages. It makes sense! But, does it make total sense; that is, is it a *True Understanding*? Just because it sounds good, does not necessarily mean you've got the entire picture – the way the Sender *intended*.

The Receiver is responsible for giving the Sender a *convincing acknowledgment*. A **convincing acknowledgement** is the Receiver's verbal and nonverbal response to the Sender's message, i.e., a reply statement, a grunt, a smile, an emphatic "no." The Sender has the right to demand a convincing acknowledgement. This is particularly important when emotions are involved in the communication process.

Another critical point is the Sender's own acknowledgement (back to the Receiver) that convinces him you got a *True Understanding* as a result of his communication to you (this may be the second cycle of communication). Note also, the Receiver does not have to agree with the Sender, but just understands what the Sender sent. However, any disagreement must be properly conveyed.

Rule #7: **The Receiver is responsible for giving the Sender a *convincing acknowledgment*.**

Scenario: Office setting – a typical exchange of greetings.
Who's Involved: Two people (Bob and Joe)

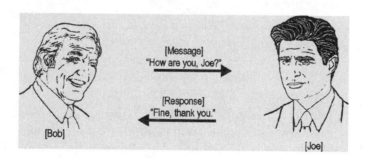

Simple enough? Let's complicate it. Suppose Joe is in a foul mood, and feeling very pessimistic. Look at the diagrams on the next page and feel the flow.

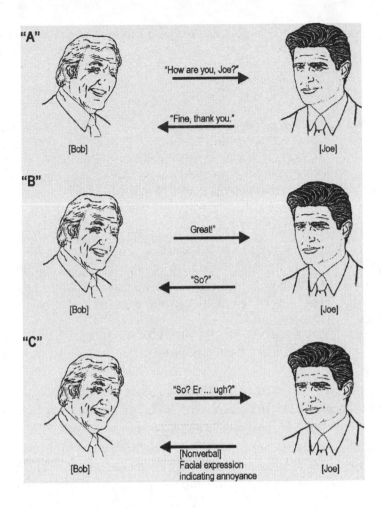

Here the receiver (Joe) did not get a *True Understanding* out of the sender's second message. Hence, a *breakdown* occurred.

Why did communication deteriorate? The original sender, Bob, sent a typical greeting message to Joe. However, Joe possibly wasn't in the mood for banality. What was Bob's intent? Whatever it was, Joe certainly did not interpret it as anything significant and rejected the communication. Bob responded with hesitation and doubt.

Simple enough? But why did the communication process deteriorate? Let's continue with the conversation.

Joe: "Do you really care how I feel today, Bob?"
Bob: "Sure." (Said with hesitation)
Joe: "Uh... I bet." (Said with doubt.)

In the next two examples of dialogue, the first is verbose, while the second conveys a *True Understanding*: swiftly, clearly, and concisely.

Scenario: Urgent data requested for meeting

Who's involved: Manager (Jack) and subordinate (Steve)

Sender (Jack):   "Oh, hi there, Steve."

Receiver (Steve): "Hi, Jack."

Jack: "How are you today?"

Steve: "Just fine, thank you."

Jack: "That's good. Listen, Steve, I need some information about the new Delta account that we got last week."

Steve: "Oh, the one Bruce Nolt landed in Wisconsin?"

Jack: "Yeah."

Steve: "What do you need?"

Jack: "Do you have an idea when we will be receiving our first order?"

Steve: "No! But possibly sometime in December, I recall."

Jack: "Well, I'm having a review meeting with the marketing folks this afternoon, and I'll need that information."

Steve: "Well, Jack, I'll see what I can come up with."

Jack: "I'd appreciate it."

Steve: "I'll call you."

Jack: "Good."

About 4:30 pm, Steve called Jack's office to let him know that the order was due around mid-December. Unfortunately for Jack, his meeting began at 4:00, and the information was not available, and Jack appeared unprepared and incompetant.

This dialogue has no hope for a *True Understanding*. It contained nonsense, lacked a sense of importance, and included a bit more "touchy-feely" interaction than necessary. It never conveyed accountability on Steve's part to provide the information promptly. As a matter of fact, it was a waste of time and money!

How would you replay the scenario? Compare your answer with the more succinct version below. You decide if a *True Understanding* is properly conveyed.

Jack: "Steve, I need to speak to you about the new Delta account."

Steve: "Sure."

Jack: "When is the first order due?"

Steve: "In December, I think, but I'll have to verify the exact date."

Jack: "I'll need that date by three this afternoon."

Steve: "Done!"

How did you do? Did you realize the need to shorten the dialogue? Can you see the benefits of creating a *True Understanding*? Jack clearly stated his intent, and Steve acknowledged accountability. The importance was conveyed by Jack. A *True Understanding* was created and properly acted upon. The option to shorten the first two statements exists as well; however, we always appreciate a little friendliness.

Lost Time

Let's talk about lost time using the previous two scenarios between Jack and Steve. The first conversation took 35 seconds, the second only 10. The difference is 25 seconds of lost time, *unproductive time*. Check the following math. Say you employ 5,000 people and during the day, each of your employees has one conversation similar to the first dialogue previously presented: 5,000 x 25 wasted seconds/day = 125,000 wasted people-seconds/day, or 35 people-hours. That adds up to 8,750 hours a year, and at $20/hour, a cost of $175,000!

And that's just the wasted time. We haven't even considered the lost productivity of inaccurate communication! Millions of dollars are lost each day in business because of the lack of accountability placed on the quality of communications. In the home, day after day, spouses, parents and children are emotionally unfulfilled because a *True Understanding* is not conveyed. In the home and office, we must take the time to learn how to say what needs to be said properly.

At work, you can have some fun. Copy the Communication Lost Time Chart in Appendix I, and let your manager or supervisor play around with it. He or she might want to buy this book! Let us be realistic. Poor communication happens daily in most companies and each could easily waste millions of dollars of company profits.

I don't recommend that everybody run around with a stop watch timing conversations, but I do recommend an increased level of awareness and quality control on communication.

Summary

True Understanding is the overriding issue. Clarifying our intent, and keeping the dialogue concise and precise is the technique.

We must always be aware of whom we are speaking with. Sometimes, we must be patient and guiding in order to get the other person to be more comfortable with the conversation.

Learn the Communication Model. Memorize it; practice it; and teach it. Learn how to confront properly. This reinforces how we communicate and focuses on generating *True Understanding* and on confronting issues as they arrive.

Rule #8:   **Take communication seriously. True Understanding is an end product, i.e., a commodity, with a price tag, and becomes a corporate or personal asset. Constantly strive for excellent communications within your companies, your families, and your relationships.**

Cycles of Communication

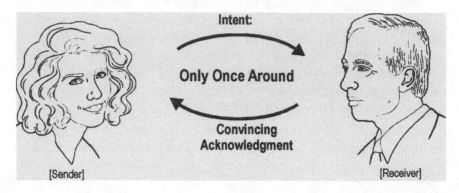

Figure 4-4: Cycles of Interpersonal Communication

As mentioned previously, our main concern is with Two-way Communication. This means that a Sender transmits to the Receiver, who in turn, acknowledges with a response to the Sender.

Step-by-step explanation:

Communication Cycle: Each time a response is completed, a Cycle is also completed. Thus each of the following dialogues is a completed cycle:

Example:

Sender:	"Good morning!"
Receiver:	Smiles [a nonverbal]
Sender:	"Everett, it's important that you call the Boston plant before 9:00 am."
Receiver :	"I agree."
Sender:	"There are just too many things to do around here!"
Receiver:	"True. Why not make a list and then prioritize them."

RULE #9: *Each cycle is complete. The conversation does not need to progress. The bottom line – If True Understanding is still required, then and only then need you proceed.*

Example: Read the following scenario:

Scenario:	Boy Meets Girl
Who's involved:	Two people

Wes:	"Hi there."
Aubree:	"Hello."
Wes:	"Would you like to go to the movies this Saturday night?"

Aubree: (hesitates) "That depends."
Wes: "On what?" (defensively)
Aubree: "What movie is playing and who I'am going with?"
Wes: (confused by her response) "Uh … Jaws?"
Aubree: "I'll call you."

The above scenario contains four complete cycles of communication:

#1   "Hi there / "Hello"
#2   "Would you like to go to the movies this Saturday night?" /"That depends."
#3   "On what?"/"What movie is playing and who I'amgoing with?"
#4   "Uh … Jaws!" / "I'll call you"

Cycle #1 is obvious: a simple statement and response.

In **cycle #2,** when Wes asked Aubree if she wanted to go the movies, he failed to communicate a *True Understanding*. Did you catch the error? He never invited her to go with him, even though he assumed she interpreted his words to mean with him. But she's going to play hard to get.

Cycle #3 could have been eliminated altogether if Wes said in Paragraph 2: "Aubree, I would like *to take* you to the movie, "Jaws," this Saturday night."

Cycle #4 needs more creativity. Wes could have displayed more confidence and enthusiasm, and invited Aubree to her choice of movies. Instead, he limited himself and possibly lost a date.

RULE #10: ***Try to get a True Understanding in each Cycle of Communication – make every effort to do so.***

RULE #11: ***It is best not to proceed with the conversation until both Sender and Receiver know exactly what is being communicated.***

It is important for you to feel comfortable with the concept of Cycle of Communication. It is critical in the Communication and Confrontation Models.

Conversation

A **Conversation** is an ongoing exchange of thoughts, opinions, and feelings. Within conversations exist many *cycles of communication*, each building upon the next.

Conversation: A series of completed Communication Cycles, each reflecting a completed True Understanding. During the conversation, the *Sender/Receiver* relationship can switch. Switching is permissible. However, the Intent of the Sender's communication needs to be honored—convincingly!

Scenario: The situation takes place in a manufacturing plant.

Who's involved: The supervisor, Bob, approaches the machine operator, Joe. Bob is in a rush and doesn't have all the facts. Joe is an ace employee and knows his work extremely well.

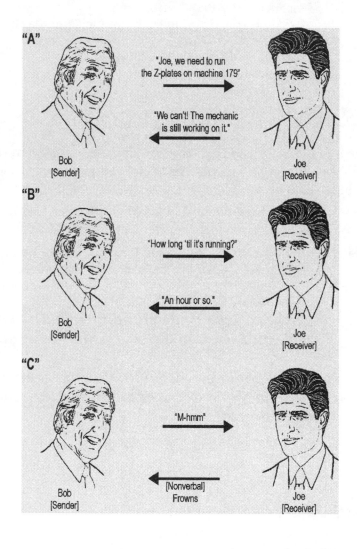

In cycle A, the supervisor's Intent could not be fulfilled. It was temporarily blocked by the broken machine. Joe's response was proper and convincing.

Cycles B and C demonstrate attempts made by Bob to gather facts. At this point, Bob no longer controlled the communication.

In cycles D and E, Joe became the sender. He was responsible for the communication cycles. This subconsciously did not cause a problem with Bob. Once Joe presented some hope to Bob, Bob's emotion (excitement) automatically kicked in, and Bob's original Intent was satisfied. In cycle F, Bob regained control of the conversation; however, Joe did manage to put his two-cents in.

Let's get a bit more critical. In cycle A, did Bob's statement support True Understanding? or provoke a communication breakdown?

Look carefully at: "Joe, we need to run the Z-plates on machine 179." No problem! Next year! The question of "When?" immediately comes to mind. Joe knew the machine's condition and properly said:

"We can't ..."

Therefore, additional communication cycles had to be made to create the True Understanding. If you investigate cycle E, you'll note that a decision was made to use machine 165. Return to Bob's original statement and ask yourself: *Why do we need to run the Z-plates on machine 179?* That was never answered. It was possible that Bob's manager gave strict orders to use only that machine because of quality issues. That issue may have been entirely lost.

Further, we really don't know Bob's Intent, and neither did Joe. But, we do know that conveying a True Understanding is the sender's responsibility. In this case, Bob may not have fulfilled his responsibility and may have become distracted when Joe found a solution to run the Z-plates quickly.

The following scenario shows how the Communication Cycle can get sidetracked and complicate matters in but a few seconds.

Scenario:	Parents are discussing how they are going to discipline their daughter, Kim.
Who's involved:	Husband, Russ, and wife, Diane

Diane:	"This morning, Kim told me that *you* restricted her from going out tonight."
Russ:	"She's definitely grounded!"
Diane:	"Why?"
Russ:	"I'm not going to change my position."
Diane:	"What did she do?"
Russ:	"Why are you defending her, Diane?"
Diane:	"I'm not, Russ. I just want to know what's going on with Kim and you."
Russ:	"Can't you leave this alone? It's between Kim and me."
Diane:	"I'm her mother, Russ!"
Russ:	"That doesn't have anything to do with Kim's punishment."

From the very start of this discussion, Diane and Russ wandered off the subject of Kim's restriction. Diane failed to present a clear *intent* and Russ may have been threatened by the "you" message and in defense took the statement for a ride. Diane never took responsibility for completing the communication cycle. Realizing Russ's comment, she could have restated or rephrased her *intent*. They instead, began attacking each other.

Diane could have started the conversation off with: "Why is Kim grounded?" This makes Russ look at Kim's restriction objectively. Unfortunately, Russ was hiding something and Diane tried to uncover it. She had to pay for it as well.

Fear

Fear is the greatest potential barrier to proper communications. It can sit directly between the sender and the receiver. Fear can be entirely the sender's own shortcoming or the receiver's own shortcoming. In either case, it's usually fear that crumbles confidence and reduces the chance of creating True Understanding.

The Communications Model addresses:

- Fear of Sending
- Fear of Receiving

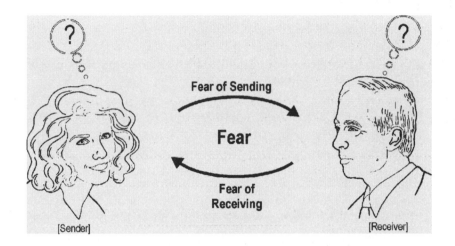

Figure 4-5: Fear

Fear of Sending: Fear of transmitting a communication with a True Understanding. Because of some **hidden** fear or phobia, the sender only <u>attempts</u> to communicate to the receiver. Due to lack of enthusiasm, True Understanding crumbles. The Intent is left *hanging*. The encoding process falters. The ability to generate a meaningful statement short-circuits. Hence, whatever sputtered out in the statement is already tainted with doubt and unable to command a True Understanding.

For example, suppose you have to speak to your boss about something important to you. But you know quite well that he or she might not want to hear about it, especially from you. So, one morning, you get ready to meet your boss and say what's on your mind. You have it rehearsed. You're all set. The boss approaches. You feel like saying something. Suddenly, it happens. That sinking feeling. You say, "Good morning," as he passes, and you go back into your corner—until next time.

Eventually, you will realize that your *intent* was left hanging and your sensory motivation was overwhelmed by your unconscious fears. As you learn the process of self-confrontation, this symptom may disappear. Your ability to self-confront keeps your intent *focused*, and that means *power*—enough power for you to say what's on your mind.

Fear of Receiving: The Receiver is afraid of hearing what he or she assumes is coming. Thus the Receiver commits a cardinal crime: *Failure to listen*. When this occurs, *the Receiver subconsciously prejudges, precludes, or alters the meaning of the message*. The ability to acknowledge convincingly is shattered. Often, this sets the stage for embarrassment, loss of respect, and the perpetuation of fear. But worst of all, this is a symptom of denial!

The less we occupy our thoughts with our fears, the more effectively we confront the issue. Practice the cardinal rule of *non-judgmental awareness*. When we abstain from prejudging the outcome, positively or negatively, we sharpen our ability to clearly present the facts and relate them to the issue. Therefore, the best way to reduce fear is to focus solely on your Intent to resolve the issue. This can be a liberating experience.

RULE #12: *When we abstain from pre-judging the outcome, positively or negatively, we sharpen our ability to clearly present the facts and relate them to the issue.*

A familiar example of fear of receiving can be seen in the previous example about your boss. Suppose you are a good worker; there's nothing obviously going wrong, but whenever your boss approaches, you tend to freeze. Your unconscious thoughts run scared. Each time he approaches, you freeze up. He says, "Good morning." Ah … all is okay, until the next time.

Since fear is common to all of us, we need not consider ourselves unique in experiencing it. As mentioned, self-confrontation eventually erases these fear-based responses, and will free you.

Note: **We cannot fully investigate this psychologically complex process of fear in the scope of this text, but, we can attempt to shed some light on this unwanted phenomenon. The Self-help section of any bookstore is full of practical advice on dealing with fear.**

Helpful guidelines to combat fear

The following may provide antidotes to fearful attitudes:

- Trust yourself and learn to trust others.
- Increase your non-judgmental awareness.
- Don't judge others personally. Behavior is all that is relevant.
- Don't pre-judge others.
- Don't pre-judge the *expected results*.

- Put energy into the purpose of the conversation.
- Be open to let the other person collaborate.
- Don't recall your failures.
- Focus on the issue.
- Focus your awareness on what the other person is up to; there is no time to daydream or think about your past during a conversation. Seek shared goals and a win-win-win outcome.

One good way to eliminate fear is to *concentrate* on the desired outcome. Always remember, the purpose of a confrontation is to resolve issues, not to cause harm and blame ourselves or others. *Focus* on the **facts**. State the facts clearly. Fear does not reside in facts. Only *truth* resides in facts. Focus on purpose.

We need not concern ourselves with the thoughts of fear and the places or times where fear can occur. We need to consciously pursue victory in the everyday battle by seeing beyond our fears. We need concern ourselves not with the idea of living out the fear, but with the immediate challenge of honor and glory of confronting the fear. We know what we have to do. We need to become more patient with ourselves, take the time to personally grow. We can overcome fear. We have to believe in ourselves, and strive for positive change.

It is without question that we achieve integrity, honor, and glory when we learn how to create and constructively deal with relationships. Our power is the ability to communicate and, if necessary, confront issues that block our desire to become an integral and fully contributing member of our society.

Let me close this chapter by including the text of an article I wrote in 1997 about what I call "Accurate Communication."

Accurate Communication: Communication Takes on a Life of Its Own

We know that interpersonal communication involves interaction between at least two people. But do we know that a higher and more sophisticated level of communications exists? I term this "Accurate Communication."

The benefits of Accurate Communication are many. When used by sales people, it shines forth the authenticity which is the backbone of building relationships with customers. When used in therapy, the subtle energies expressed reveal whether or not clients are speaking their truth. And in every interaction, what is said earns respect and radiates confidence.

Accurate Communication connotes that your total-self is participating when you are speaking, that is, your mind, body, spirit or soul. By "total-self," I mean all aspects of your-self including your soul or spirit and your subconscious mind. It's beyond rational thought, and includes "intuitive" dialogue that is generated from the total-self perspective.

Accurate Communication means speaking from your HEART, from the highest regions of the mind and from the depths of the soul. There's nothing hidden, everything is expressed!

When you speak "accurately," your voice tone and bodily vibration carries a sustaining vibration that the listener more readily accepts. When a person does not speak well, people tend to pull away and not take that person too seriously. Accurate Communication implies that what is being spoken flows from the speaker as sincere and complete. In turn, what is heard by the listener is more completely received. Unfortunately, I need to put in this caution: please be aware of those actors and con-artists who speak not from their truth. Accurate Communication is a relationship building process and we need to always know with whom we are associating.

What does Accurate Communication feel like? When you speak in this state, both your intellectual mind" (the mental aspect) and your "emotional mind" (the heart-felt aspect) become more in balance. You are not speaking solely rationally nor solely emotionally, but by combining the two centers, a third or composite voice is manifested. It's like hearing music with headphones on rather than in a large room with speakers. With headphones, the music surrounds you and fills the entire audio space, whereas with speakers, you are apart from the music and can be distracted by noise.

In a balanced state, intuition improves, and you will feel what is true to you. If you say something that is not true to you, you will feel a hesitation or a discomfort. When you speak authentically, you are saying what is intuitively true in the moment as you perceive it to be. Bear in mind, it doesn't matter if what you are saying is true or not, right or wrong. What is important is being authentic as you perceive yourself to be.

Speaking accurately also means that your left-brain intellectual function and your right-brain intuitive functions are in balance with each other, and in balance with your emotional heart-mind. These three form what I term the "personal human trinity."

When you speak at the personal human trinity level, you resonate with conviction, confidence, and wisdom. According to Dr. Victor Beasley, author of Intuition By Design, it's at this point where you are using the "Intelligence of the Heart," that is, "intuition and intellect bonded in a blissful marriage within one's own consciousness." It is here that the listener can discern the level of integrity and wisdom behind what the speaker is saying.

When the personal human trinity exists within both the speaker and the listener during a dialog, the relationship is in balance and carries its own identity or relational human trinity. This is when dialogue and true understanding flourish. Both speaker and listener are in balance and the relationship strengthens.

The benefits of the relational human trinity are profound. It brings authenticity and integrity into the relationship, and fosters growth and openness. A win-win-win condition exists in which the speaker, the listener, and the relationship succeed, with accuracy and intuition at their peaks.

Speaking and listening accurately are key for those dedicated to self-mastery and human development. Our world and our relationships depend on how we communicate with others, and it's imperative to present yourself as accurately and authentically to the best of your potential.

To help you become an Accurate Communicator, I've listed twelve basic steps. The more you practice each step, the better the outcome. You'll feel more confident because you are bringing respect into the communication process. And when you do this, the relationship flourishes. Practice each step until you have embedded it into your normal communication routine, and you will have a life-long skill.

1. **Desire and Visualize what you want to say.** Envision your desire in picture form with has much detail as possible, including the desired outcome.

2. **Set your Intent**. What exactly is your intent? (e.g. "I desire to speak from the core of my heart, to express my love to you.")

3. **Expand your Consciousness**. This important step connects you to your "higher-self" and ensures balance in what you will communicate into the relationship. To do this, take a deep breath, center and feel your essence, then raise your consciousness at least three feet above your head.

4. **Do not prejudge the conversation or the outcome.** Do not put expectations or rationale onto the potential of the conversation. Instead, formulate what would be beneficial to the conversation and stay focused on that.

5. **Center yourself to open up to your own intuition.** Intuition could be said to be: "knowing something previously unknown, and knowing that it is now known." When in balance, permit intuition to flow through you as if your higher-self was doing the talking.

6. **Stay focused in the 'now' to enhance your perception of the transmission.** Stay focused and permit your senses to assist you. Reading nonverbal signals and facial expressions heighten your perceptive powers and help you better understand what is being transmitted and received.

7. **Ascertain that the receiver has granted you attention.** It's best to have 100% attention from the receiver before proceeding with any conversation. The less attentive the receiver, the more will be lost in the dialogue.

8. **Be precise with your wording.** Extra words only add extra noise to interpret. Keep it simple and clear.

9. **Feel that what is being said comes from your heart.** When it comes from the heart, it feels sincere and reflects your total being. If it comes solely from the intellect, it could be cold and without compassion.

10. **Listen attentively to yourself as you speak each word.** Reaffirm that what you are saying is necessary to your intent. Make sure that what you say respectfully gets the point across.

11. **Receive acknowledgment that you been correctly understood.** Make sure the listener understood you. Look for a response that assures you that you are both talking the same talk.

12. **Self-confirm that your intent, communicated and acknowledged, has been manifested and is now complete.** Once the dialogue has been completed, verify that your intent has been properly conveyed and addressed. Your conversation is now complete. Feel *balanced* and sense your *wholeness*. Feel joy!

In summary, Accurate Communications means balance with our mind, intellect, and heart. It is intuitively driven, resonates authenticity, and provides opportunity for wisdom to shine forth. Both speaker and listener can apply these skills, and in so doing, they can create their own personal human trinity. Once accomplished, the relationship becomes its own entity and thus forms a relational human trinity. As each of us experiences speaking accurately, we find that it also applies to listening. Relationships based on accurate communication are major components of self-mastery.

The Confrontation Model

The next step to take the fear out of facing others is to learn confronting skills. Confrontation is an issue-resolving and problem-solving skill—a tool for su pervisors, managers, parents, teachers, nurses, teenagers; in effect, it's for everybody! It is a process which provides you with **instant feedback**. It is a valuable and useful way of getting things done and eliminating problems.

Many cultures, especially the Chinese, view the concept of confrontation as hostile and improper. However, Chinese engineers and nurses working in the U.S. who completed confrontation classes felt more empowered and adjusted in their jobs. Prior to the course, they avoided confrontation.

The Confrontation Model emphasizes *building upon the relationship*, and eschews any form of combat or hostility. In fact, our use of the model leads to spiritual growth as we foster better and workable relationships. The model mitigates the conflicts which impede relationships and cleans the mind from laboring issues which bog us down, suppress our creativity, and hinder relationship enrichment. In fact, the third "Win" in "Win–Win–Win" refers to the fact that your relationship also wins in a successful confrontation.

So, let's get down to business. First, the terminology. The following terms will help you better understand the process of confrontation. They apply to most everyday situations.

Problem: Something that needs to be corrected or changed, such as attitudinal and behavioral changes, work performance, and disrespect. Problems have two components: causes and symptoms. Remember, correcting symptoms does not help; you must eliminate the cause of the problem.

Cause: The root of the problem; the concern or reason for which something has undergone change and is now causing a problem.

Symptom: A sign, condition, by-product; or temporary event which often appears to be a problem, but isn't. However, when remedied, the problem reappears with other symptoms. The process of eliminating symptoms leads you to the most identifiable cause.

Problem-solving: The two-step process of identifying 1) the scope of the problem, and 2) determining why it is a problem.

Issue: The essential point or matter of discussion, debate, or dispute. Think of an issue as what is *between* the confronter and confrontee, with resolving it as the object of the confrontation.

The issue may be a problem, a concern, an attitude, or a behavior. Ideally, an issue addresses a problem's most **identifiable cause**. Dealing with the Issue is one of the most important functions of management. Think of a problem as something *concrete* from which an issue has evolved.

Intent: A succinct statement of the purpose and goal of the communication. The reason behind the action. The causal or driving reason. It is the mind's energizing force to create or change something. By invoking the intent, the confrontee receives a clear understanding as to the desired win-win-win outcome.

Collaboration: The communication process in which two parties with an interest in reaching a win-win-win resolution work together intelligently toward mutual agreement. Collaboration is taking a position in which input from both confronter and confrontee is valued.

Collaboration is a process which fosters creative and intuitive dialogue; it also provides encouragement to the participants of the conversation.

Confrontation: To come face-to-face with an issue, a person, or a group to address an issue. It is accomplished with great awareness and discipline.

Confrontation does not mean to physically fight or to go into armed combat. It simply means that something which needs to be *changed* or *corrected* will, in fact, *get changed* in order to resolve the issue. The Confrontation Model is a process which shows you how to get things changed.

Confrontor: The person who identifies that an issue needs to be resolved. The person who initiates the confrontation; the one in control; the person who addresses issues and enforces a collaborative resolution of issues or problems. The person who sets the Confrontation Model in motion.

Confrontee: The person being confronted; generally, this is the person directly accountable for resolving the issue or problem.

The following scenario offers a better understanding of these basic terms:

Scenario: Machine shop operator's productivity
Who's Involved: Supervisor (Ron) and Operator (Jane)

When Ron, the supervisor, checked the latest weekly productivity report, he realized that one of his most highly productive presses, #179, had low output. Jane operates machine #179. Its current efficiency is 67% but it should be about 88%.

Ron checked several other reports to verify or to find causes for #179's low production: maintenance, supplies, materials, down time, etc. Nothing provided the reason for the low efficiency. Ron pulled out Jane's performance profile and it indicated high machine efficiencies, except for the last week.

With these facts, Ron approaches Jane. He confronts her with the issue of low machine efficiency.

> Ron opens with "Jane, did you know that 179's productivity was way low last week?"
>
> Jane retorts: "I know it's lower; but it's too hot in the mill. I'm getting tired quickly."
>
> [Ron listens carefully to Jane's response, and interprets it as a symptom, but not necessarily the cause of, low productivity.]
>
> "Jane," says Ron, "you've always performed well despite the heat."
>
> Jane grins, hesitates, then says, "Yeah." [Ron gets the feeling that Jane knows the answer, but remains silent.]
>
> Ron says, "The issue is the need to improve 179's efficiency. Jane, what can be done about it?"

Let's stop the confrontation scenario at this point to analyze the confrontation:

Issue:	Machine 179's productivity needs to improve
Confronter:	Ron
Confrontee:	Jane
Problem:	Currently, Jane's poor performance
Cause:	Unknown.
Symptom:	Jane's claim: "...it's too hot.."
Problem-solving:	Ron's efforts to identify low machine efficiency, gather facts, investigate symptoms, and seek to find the causes.

3-phase Approach to the Confrontation Model

Experience gained from the many people who have used the Confrontation Model shows that you might initially be defensive or intimidated by its power and directness. You might either rush into confronting every issue in your life, or feel overwhelmed and reject the model and its techniques.

To avoid either situation, we will use a three-phase learning process to ease into the model comfortably and systematically without intimidation.

1. *De-programming* — first accept that your way of confronting may be problematic and stressful. The psychological and behavioral scripting that you may have used in the past has not served you and must evolve. But do not be discouraged. Very few people can do this naturally. The De-Programming Phase is critical. It allows for the psychological adjustments to be made as you learn the power behind the model.

2. *Scripting*—here's where you incorporate the basic techniques of the model with the understanding that it serves to build relationships. By this stage, you will have relinquished most of your fears about using the techniques. Constant repetition and replay of each technique reinforces your ability to concentrate on the issue and coach the confrontee towards a win-win-win outcome.

3. *Personalizing*. By now, you will have obtained a solid level of comfort and confidence using the techniques. Now you begin to modify the techniques to some extent in order to personalize them or feel comfortable with your verbal and nonverbal style.

Phase One: De-Programming

Before you attempt to employ the Confrontation Model's techniques, it is best to record how you actually confront issues based on your current abilities. If at all possible, ask a friend to make an audio or video tape of you confronting someone. Should you not have access to these high-tech devices, then try to jot down how you feel about the way you recently confronted someone, or yourself for that matter.

Ask the following questions:

- What was my intent in confronting?
- Did I clearly state the issue?
- Was I accurate with what I communicated?
- Did I stay focused?
- Did this confrontation serve me?
- How can I improve my confrontation techniques?
- Did the confrontee feel good about being confronted?
- Did the issue get resolved?
- What did I learn from this confrontation?

Students of our classes go through several video-taped exercises in which they realize the ineffectiveness of their confrontation abilities. Once this realization is made, however, they are eager to learn the Confrontation Model.

Phase Two: Scripting

Scripting provides learners with the opportunity to reprogram their responses using the techniques of the Confrontation Model. The best result is obtained when you accept and trust the model as it is presented. Don't hunt for its shortcomings. Seek what it offers and learn the psychological significances of its components and strategy.

As you incorporate these techniques into your responses, you are replacing your old useless scripts. Now, the more you practice the components of each technique, you will also replace your bodily-oriented scripts (your behaviors). As you will soon find out, incorporating a technique called the "1–2–3 Approach" is no easy task. But once you have practiced it enough and overriden your old script with this technique, you will realize the power of "focusing" you have gained. Scripting the 1–2–3

Approach technique is empowerment and serves to free you from hesitation, doubt, and fear. You have befriended the power of capturing time and space while demonstrating the skill of concentration. This by no means can be taken lightly—you have changed!

Phase Three: Personalizing

Personalizing comes after mastery of the Confrontation Model's techniques. To pre-maturely personalize the model's techniques will most likely be a disservice to you and weaken your abilities to effectively confront others. By prematurely personalizing, you may very well be protecting an unconscious fear. This will erode your confidence. It's better to be able to know the basics and let this knowledge serve as your foundation. It's important not to camouflage the basics with premature personalizing.

How to personalize the Confrontation Model techniques is addressed in "Advanced Confrontation Techniques," (Chapter 8). We recommend that you learn the model well before you modify it with your personal verbal and non-verbal styles.

The Confrontation Model

At this time, let's introduce the Confrontation Model. It is presented as seven figures, each building upon the previous one. The Confrontation Model's fundamental design is that of a pyramid. We chose to use the graphic concept of the pyramid for several reasons. First, it's ascending to new heights. Second, it contains hidden treasures and artifacts inside while demanding careful attention as you climb the outside. And third, most people are mystified and fascinated by the Great Pyramids. We believe that as you experience the Confrontation Model's pyramid, you will not only find resolution to your issues, but will find treasures about yourself. Before the journey outward can succeed, the journey inward must be taken.

The model has important primary *components*, and as each new component appears, it is printed in **bold type** and backdropped by gray shading.

Figure 5.1 portrays an ascending dialogue to the Summit Goals. The journey up the pyramid connotes a *to-and-fro* interaction between the confronter and the confrontee. The slopes are manageable. If too steep, the confrontation dialogue becomes too difficult—someone will fall off. If the slopes are too flat, little is communicated and change is unlikely to occur.

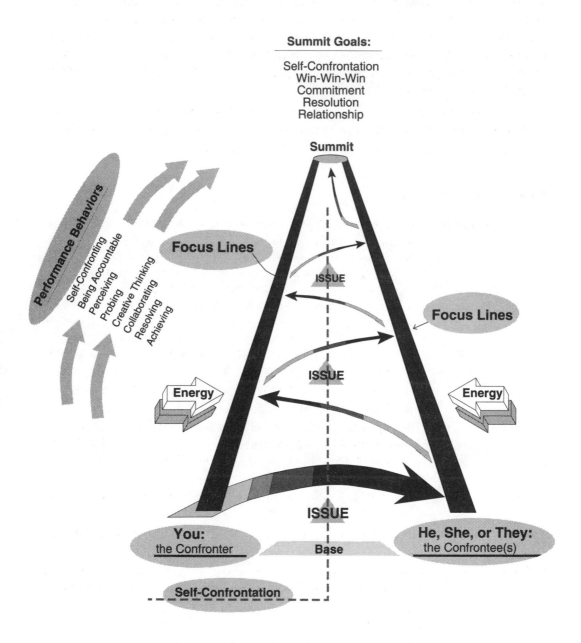

Figure 5-1 The Confrontation Model — the Pyramid Concept

The confronter and confrontee both release and exchange energy, and this must be channeled properly. If one overpowers the other, someone is going to back off and fall. If insufficient energy is exchanged, there may be insufficient intent to resolve the *issue*. The *issue* contains the purpose and focus of the confrontation. The Confrontation Model centralizes the *issue* and maintains its objectivity throughout the confrontation process. Whenever the *issue* fades from focus and Intent, confrontation loses its power and disintegrates.

Eight interdependent Performance Behaviors effectively measure a behavioral quality or characteristic of the confronter. These behaviors provide instant feedback to the confronter, during or after a confrontation interaction.

Performance Behaviors

Self-Confronting: A pre-confrontation self-assessment. Before going into a confrontation using the Confrontation Model techniques, the confronter examines the worth and practicality of the confrontation. He or she reflects for a moment and ascertains that confronting the *issue* is justifiable. It is a time to humble the ego by making sure that the confrontation will not be an attack on the other person but rather serve as a way to resolve an issue and build upon the relationship. Self-confronting is a time of personal empowerment and final review of the issue and facts prior to the actual confrontation.

Accountability: The confronter decides that the situation must be resolved and that he or she is the appropriate person to do that.

Perceiving: The confronter's role in making sense of the circumstances surrounding the issue; identifying the verbal and nonverbal behaviors of the confrontee; being aware of yourself and how you are being perceived by the confrontee

Probing: Penetrating the facts and seeking out information; not being easily satisfied or distracted by the confrontee

Creative Thinking: Being alert and imaginative; open to your gut-level *intuitive* feelings; not being overcome by doubt

Collaborating: Listening; being patient; not telling nor prompting confrontee's defensiveness; receptive to the confrontee's creative thoughts

Resolving: Staying focused on how the *issue* can be mutually responded to and taken care of

Achieving: Feeling success, the mental and physical sensation of knowing that you are making progress in your confrontation

Figure 5-1 Step-by-step explanation:

Pyramid: The confrontation model concept. The mental arena wherein the activities of confrontation must always take place. Before you confront, the concept board of the pyramid must be invoked.

You: The *Confronter*, the person who seeks to address an issue and confront another person or group.

They: The *Confrontee(s)*, the person or group responsible for responding and for taking corrective action. The confrontee has been designated to be accountable for achieving problem resolution.

Issue: The object of the confrontation. A succinct discussion about a behavior, event, job task, or skill which must undergo change to bring about the desired outcome.

Focus Lines: The slopes of the pyramid which the confrontation dialogue must never cross over. Remember: Always keep the conversation topic confined within the Focus Lines.

Summit Goals

Figure 5-2 shows that mutually reaching the Summit Goals accomplishes five major things:

1. We confront our procrastinations and fears, and face the pending *issue*
2. We arrive at a Win-Win-Win situation in which both parties are satisfied, *and* the relationship prospers
3. We lay the foundation for resolving the *issue* by honoring personal commitment and integrity
4. We witness change and the resolution of the *issue* to bring about the desired outcome
5. We establish the attitudes and conditions for improving the effectiveness and depth of the relationship.

To empower the confrontation dialogue, the confronter must place emphasis on the "mutual" attainment of the ultimate resolution. This keeps the intent of the dialogue intact. Keeping a mutual orientation serves to intrinsically motivate the confronter and the confrontee. Figure 5-2 illustrates the Summit Goals components:

Rule #13:   **Keep the Issue sparate from the Confrontee as much as possible, especially at the onset of the confrontation.**

Rule #14:   **"You" and "they" are confronting the Issue, not confronting each other.**

Rule #15:   **Don't personalize the Issue or the confrontation.**

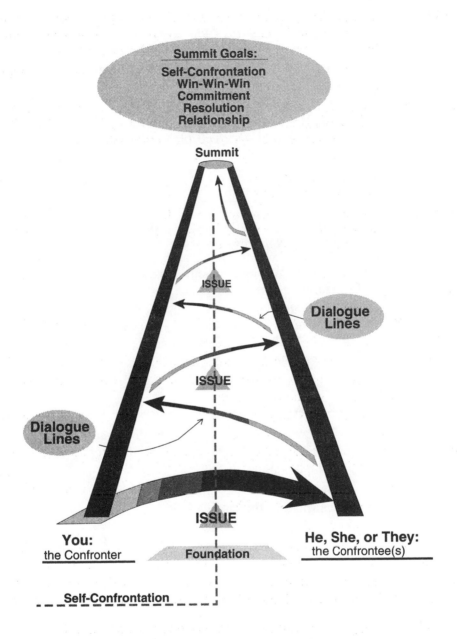

Figure 5-2: The Confrontation Model - Summit Goals

Figure 5-2 Step-by-Step Explanation

Self-Confrontation: Eliminating your own fears and emotions precedes confronting others. When this is accomplished, you will feel more confident and empowered to continue with the confrontation process.

Win-Win-Win: The end result to which the confrontee is directed. Then, the confrontee realizes that he has created a resolution of the issue in which *everyone wins*, including the relationship.

Commitment: The confrontee should willingly state that he will follow-through with the agreement negotiated. The integrity of the confrontee is upheld. The confrontee has fully participated in the resolution and corrective action. Commitment is a very powerful psychological tool. Obtaining commitment from the confrontee is the second most difficult task for the confronter to perform.

Resolution: The resolution occurs whenever the confronter and confrontee ascertain that the *issue* has been completely resolved. Actually, both should share in the glory of this moment, regardless of the degree of importance. The resolution can be accomplished some time after the confrontation.

Relationship: Building and renewing the relationship is the ultimate goal of the confrontation process. We confront in order to resolve issues and build relationships. This human quality expands our personal and social potential and well being.

☐ Self-Learning Review Exercise:

a.   What's the difference between a *symptom* and a *cause*?
b.   Define the term *issue*.
c.   What does "collaboration" mean?
d.   Explain the term "confronting an issue."
e.   Explain the purpose of the Focus Lines.
f.   What's the intent of the Pyramid?
g.   Explain the concept "Win-Win-Win."
h.   What is meant by the term "resolution"?
i.   What is meant by the Rule: "Keep the *issue* separate from the confrontee as much as possible..."?

The 1–2–3 Approach

Figure 5-3 illustrates the 1–2–3 Approach.

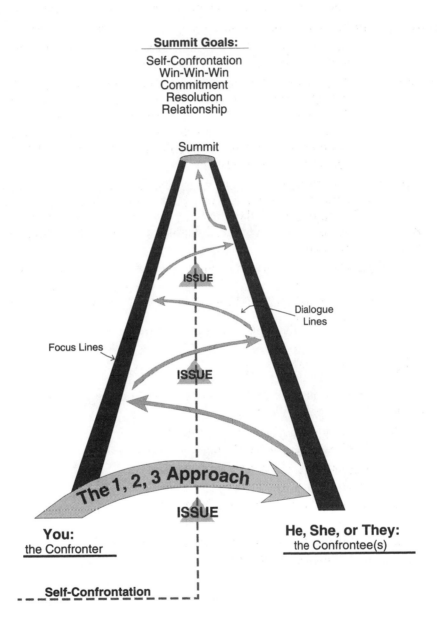

Figure 5-3: The Confrontation Model— The 1–2–3 Approach

Step-by-step explanation:

The 1-2-3 Approach: The most important aspect of the Confrontation Model is the three-part opening Dialogue Line:

1. **The Introduction (Intro)**
2. **The Clear Concise Statement (C.C.S.)**
3. **The Fix**

You must know how to use this approach expertly! *It is the **soul** of the Confrontation Model. The 1-2-3 Approach sets the confrontation process into action. It must be done correctly; otherwise, you will probably encounter obstacles which could have been avoided.* Practice the 1-2-3 Approach until it's part of your thoughts and is automatic as your breath.

Let's look at each of the three strategic components:

1 **The Intro**: Your initial act of getting the other person's or group's attention. Examples: "Joe, I'd like to speak with you." "Hi there, folks!" "Rich, there's something that I must talk to you about." Make sure you have the confrontee's full attention. If not, repeat your Intro using more emphasis, that is, stronger voice, eye contact, and body language.

Rule #16:   *Do not proceed beyond the Intro unless you get 100% attention from the confrontee(s).*

2 **The Clear Concise Statement**: A brief statement of the *issue* to the confrontee. You must get your point across in eight words or less, such as:

- "You have been late three times this week."
- "Okay, kids, we're leaving in five minutes."
- "Joe, performance needs improvement."
- "Productivity of machine 179 dropped."
- "Joanne complained about sexual harassment — again!"

Rule #17:   *Use eight (8) words or less for the C.C.S.*

The shorter the better. Keep the C.C.S. as short and to the point as possible. The purpose of the C.C.S. is to emphasize that the responsibility of the problem or issue belongs to the confrontee. This must be accomplished as *clearly* and *swiftly* as possible.

3 **The Fix**: The catalyst statement that sets the confrontation in motion. Strategically, The Fix puts ***accountability*** into action. It makes things ***happen***. The Fix activates one or more of the following psychological orientations:

- The conscious mind: the confrontee's awareness to the issue
- The sub-conscious mind: the confrontee's search for the relationship between the *issue* and his past experiences
- The unconscious mind: the confrontee's inability to identify or relate to the *issue*
- The "squirm factor:" the confrontee's realization of accountability for the *issue*, which in most cases is demonstrated by physical discomfort or excessive body movements

The *principle statement, premise or proposition* used for the Fix in the Confrontation Model is:

"What are you going to do about it?"

Simple enough? Well, you might think so, but how many times have you tried it before? Most people bypass this propositional statement and instead, **tell** the other person what to do. Which, in the end, only causes the other person to defend himself more and utter rebuttals.

When a statement like:

"What are you going to do about it?"

(or any statement which infers a similar meaning) is invoked, the confronter passes to the confrontee the psychological transfer of accountability to create and solve the intent behind the *issue*. The confronter formally informs the confrontee that the resolution of the *issue* must be the responsibility of the confrontee, who takes on ownership of that responsiblity.

During this process, the confronter releases his or her responsibility to solve the *issue*, unless, of course, the confrontee can provide more facts which the confronter needs to further evaluate. The Fix statement has profound implications for the confrontee, and this process shouldn't be taken lightly.

People have the most trouble with the Fix. One of the main reasons for this shortcoming is fear of *Rebuttal* (see later).

Why is the Fix at the *on-set* of confrontation so crucial?

... because the Fix serves as the breaking-away point!

Suppose you are the confronter. At what point in the Confrontation Model do you expect the confrontee to realize that he or she is accountable for the issue and create a resolution?

Now let's turn this around. Suppose you are the confront*ee*. At what point in the Confrontation Model would you expect the confronter to *ask* you to be accountable for the issue and create a resolution?

The only logical and rational place is at the *Fix*, the breaking point which divides two very important elements of **responsibility**:

> (1) The confronter is accountable to confront the confrontee, *and*
> (2) The confrontee is accountable to confront the issue.

The only other sensible place where the Fix appears is when it must be repeated after *Rebuttals.*

Finally, we need to discuss the use of the word "you" when stating the Fix. Good communicators, when addressing the topics of listening skills and conflict resolution techniques, often advocate avoiding the word "you." The "I" message is preferred.

In the Confrontation Model, invoking the Fix is a most critical procedure and requires utmost care, diplomacy, strategy and respect for the confrontee because the confronter, in essence, is about to transfer ("to dump" literally speaking) a potentially difficult task upon the confrontee. Caution should be taken. If the "you" can skillfully be avoided and be effective, then use another word.

Rule #18:   ***Your fundamental concern in the Fix is to protect the transfer of accountability and return proper resolution of the issue to the Confrontee.***

Study the following samples of the Fix (the use of "you" implies the confrontee):

- "What are you going to do about it, Tom?"
- "I don't want to see this happen again."
- "How are you going to resolve the Issue, Joe?"
- "When do you expect to resolve this matter?"
- "When should I expect this to be done?"
- "Helen, the issue is wearing inappropriate clothing. Can that be corrected?"
- "How can we change this, John?"
- "I would like to see something done about it, Jane."
- "Will you see that this gets accomplished?"
- "I appreciate immediate action, Tom, so that this issue gets resolved."
- "Joe, how can you best handle this situation?"
- "We can work together on this issue. However, I expect cooperation on your part. Okay?"
- "Are we agreed as to what needs to be done?"
- "Let me know if my assistance is needed."
- "You are a very good employee, and I feel that this issue can easily be corrected."

Some of you may feel more comfortable by adding the following words to the beginning of the Fix:

"Now, I need to ask you…"

Tying the 1–2–3 Approach together, we get something like this when dealing with a worker's repeated tardiness:

"Hi Mary. There's something we need to talk about."...
(pause) "Tardiness!" ... (read her nonverbals and body language).
"Now, I need to ask what you are going to do about it."

Bear in mind that the Fix must follow the C.C.S. If you allow anything more than a brief pause, the confrontee can assume control of the confrontation. Be prepared to state the Fix with as much intensity as the Intro and C.C.S.

Once the C.C.S has been delivered, the confrontee's mind vigorously begins to work. The essence of The Fix is the focus of accountability and action, and unfortunately — reaction! Here are some possible confrontee reactions:

Conscious Mind says:	Creative Subconscious Mind says:
The search begins.	"Is it true?"
The hunt is on.	"How should I approach this?"
Too much pressure.	"I'll counter-attack!"
Seeking the truth.	"I'm accountable."

Return to Figure 5-3 and look at the Confrontation Model. Where does the 1–2–3 Approach begin? If you said at the lower left (you), you're right. Otherwise, you are being confronted!

Remember, you have now started climbing to the Summit. Get ready for the confrontee's to respond.

Exercise: Stand in front of a mirror and say:

"Hi (your name) ... There's something we need to talk about ... Your
ability to confront others" ... (Read your nonverbals and body language)
"What are you going to do about it?"

Repeat until you've reached a good consistent flow. Next, ask a friend or family member (children are great) to take the place of the mirror, i.e., be the confrontee. Ask him or her to say whatever comes to mind. But do not proceed after the Fix. Stop! Repeat and practice until you are comfortable standing face-to-face with another person.

A final word on the 1–2–3 Approach. You'll soon realize that getting into position and standing within 5 feet (ideally, 3 feet) in front of the confrontee is, in of itself, a challenging task. How and what you say in the 1–2–3 Approach depends on how comfortable you are and how you present yourself.

Pre-positive Intro

Once you are comfortable with the 1–2–3 Approach, you can personalize the process. Enhancing the process depends on your personal style and behavior.

A **Pre-positive Introduction** prefixes the Intro. It may be:

- A compliment
- A good-will phrase or gesture
- A brief narrative or conversation
- A positive orientation toward the *issue* soon to be confronted
- A pre-negotiation dialogue
- Or just a friendly chat

Wisely used, pre-positive introductions serve to bridge the relationship, adjust attitudes, and set the pace and manner (positioning) of the confrontation dialogue soon to be presented.

Example:

You need to ask your boss about taking an extra day off. The boss's predictable rebuttal might relate your job current demands rather than anything personal. Your *issue* is **time-off,** and your approach may go as follows:

1 *The pre-positive introduction:*

"Hi, Sam. How are things going for you this busy week."
"Oh, hectic as usual."
"Yea, me too, but I've got a good handle on it."

The Intro:

"By the way, Sam, I need to mention something important to you."
"What's that?"

2 *The C.C.S.:*

"I need to take next Tuesday off ..."

3 *The Fix:*

"... I hope we can work it in for me."

Our ability to use some form of pre-positive introduction statement invariably depends on our confidence and ability to use the 1–2–3 Approach consistently.

Rule #19: *"The Shorter the Better."*

As a reminder, it is important to prepare yourself to undergo the Scripting phase at this time. Learn the basics and you will see there is plenty of room for you to Personalize many of the model techniques. But first build a solid and confident foundation on which you can rely. That will serve you well—trust the model.

Confrontation Discomfort

For many reasons, you may be uncomfortable in initiating a confrontation:

- Fear that you might upset the confrontee
- Fear that you'll put the confrontee on the spot and make him or her uncomfortable
- Fear that the confrontee will reject you and end your relationship
- Fear that you'll fail in managing the confrontation and appear to be a weak manager, spouse, parent, child, etc.

The whole purpose of the Confrontation Model is to get rid of the fear and resolve issues. Practice makes perfect, and the more you apply the Confrontation Model, the less discomfort you will feel. If you ever played golf, remember the first time you swung a club? Awkward and uncomfortable. The same goes for the Confrontation Model; soon you will see that the benefits of its use will overcome your fears and you'll play the confronting game with confidence.

The Rebuttal

See Figure 5-4 for the components of the Rebuttal.

Figure 5-4 Step-by-step explanation:

Rebuttal #1:   Expect any kind of response from the receiver: a denial, defensiveness, an exaggeration, an emotional reaction (tears), a question, a vulgarity, a statement of fact, or even an agreement.

Fact #1:   A simple statement of provable fact.

There are three variations of the Rebuttal:

1. Negative and challenging
2. Positive, though, challenging (indicates potential collaboration)
3. In agreement and committed to change

The order presented above depicts the probability of the kind of Rebuttal you'll receive. A key to successful confrontations is to be prepared (emotionally as well as rationally) at all times to properly respond to the Rebuttal. For instance, should a confrontee's Rebuttal be in agreement, make sure you affirm and compliment the individual. Then proceed to the Goals (Win-Win-Win, Commitment, and the Resolution).

Avoid assuming that the response will be negative, positive, or agreement. There have been times when the confronter receives a favorable Rebuttal but, assuming that he will get a negative Rebuttal, fails to move quickly to closure. When a confrontee attempts to favorably collaborate and the confronter doesn't, emotions arise and the *focus* of the issue is shattered.

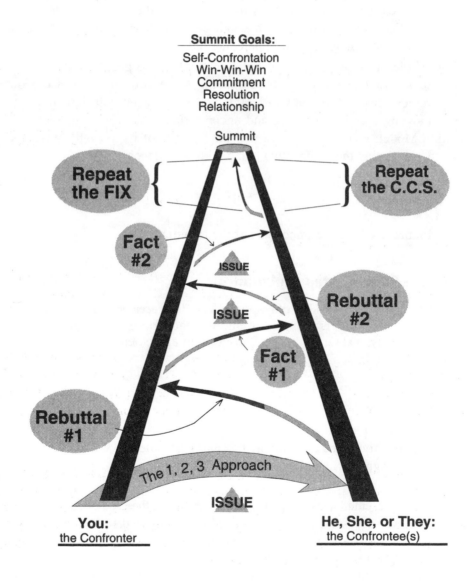

Figure 5-4: The Confrontation Model — Rebuttal

Don't get caught in an emotional trap fail to listen, or prejudge a Rebuttal. Listen carefully and be ready, and above all, *don't get emotional!*

Rule #20: **Simply state only one fact to support your position on the issue. Do not rattle-off a series of facts.**

This is one of the most abused rules. If the confronter *violates* this rule, the following can happen:

- He will lose control
- The confrontee may realize how much the confronter really does or doesn't know
- The confronter gives the confrontee a few extra moments of time to think about a counter-strategy.

Remember: *Stating one fact at a time is a critically important offensive position and strategy.*

Rebuttal #2: This is the second attempt by the confrontee to justify his position. It could very well be a repeat of Rebuttal #1. In many cases, you will find agreement and understanding at this point. Proceed to Win-Win-Win.

Fact #2: This is the confronter's second opportunity to state ONE more supportive fact. The same rules apply here as in Fact #1.

Regaining Focus of Intent

The confrontee, if challenging, will attempt to break your confidence and focus. If you intuitively sense this, there are two excellent techniques you can use:

- Repeat the Fix
- Repeat the C.C.S.

The confrontee soon gets the message that you know what he or she is thinking. Then the strategy that he or she is using deteriorates. This can force the ego to back down, humble up, and seek the truth. You'll enjoy the simplicity of this process for your intuition accelerates and your perception of the confrontation dialogue improves.

Repeat the Fix

If the confronter is *not* gaining any ground after the second or third Fact, repeat the exact same Fix statement used at the beginning of the confrontation. This starts the entire confrontation process over again. It informs the confrontee that you are not satisfied with his or her progress to this point. The *subliminal message* is clear: I (the confronter) am not persuaded by your (the confrontee) rebuttals, and now demand your honesty and acceptance to resolve the Issue.

Repeat the C.C.S.

Repeat the C.C.S. also helps the Confronter to stay focused and keep the Confrontee focused as well. To apply either one of these two application techniques, observe the following rules:

Rule #21: **Repeat the Fix when the confrontee tries to escape accountability for resolving the issue yet has already admitted or acknowledged ownership. The confrontee attempts to manipulate facts or control the dialogue.**

Rule #22: **Repeat the C.C.S. whenever the confronter (you) or the confrontee losses focus of the issue. Repeating the C.C.S. invariably brings the issue back in focus.**

Duration of the Confrontation

The duration of the confrontation is usually independent of the magnitude of the issue. You may have a very simple issue, but a very stubborn employee, spouse, or child. Hence, the potential for a drawn out confrontation exists. However, the more skill you have, the less time you will spend in a confrontation.

Time Line: To establish reasonable duration of confrontations, adhere to the following guidelines:

Degree of Confrontation Difficulty	*Time Needed*
1. Easy	30 seconds
2. Average to moderate	70-90 secs
3. Moderate to difficult	2 minutes
4. Very difficult	Over 2 minutes

Please remember that these are only guidelines. A very difficult confrontation can last only a few seconds. An example of a difficult and advanced confrontation that took just 12 seconds follows:

Scenario: The CEO and V.P. of Manufacturing regarding bonuses.

CEO: "John, the issue of production bonuses this year is dead!"

V.P.: "Phil, let me remind you, the real issue is that you have publicly committed to give bonuses this year."

CEO: "You're right, John. I did."

This example reflected an "advanced, personalized" application of the Confrontation Model. It succinctly applied the 1–2–3 Approach, a Rebuttal, and a Resolution.

The Overshoot and Undershoot

See Figure 5-5 for the components of the Overshoot and Undershoot.

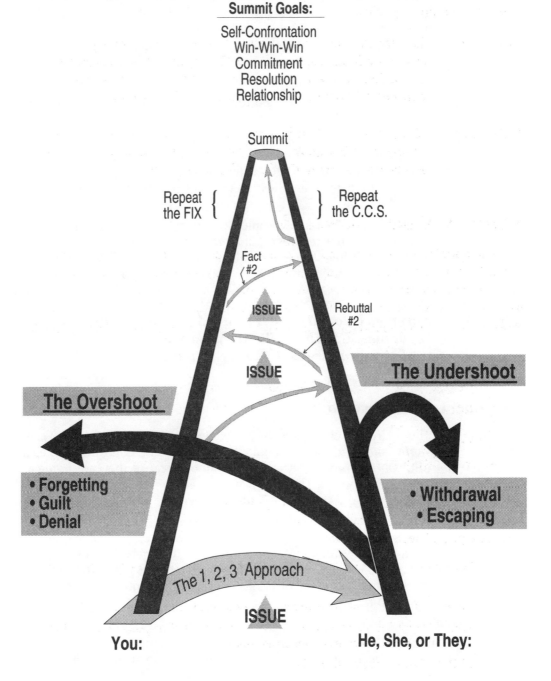

Figure 5-5: The Confrontation Model—the Overshoot and Undershoot

Figure 5-5 Step-by-step explanation:

Overshoot: Occurs when the confrontee evades the 1–2–3 Approach with *overt* offensive behavior. Actually, the Rebuttal #1 line attempts to take the conversation outside of the pyramid while throwing the accountability for resolution back to the confronter.

    The confrontee tries to avoid responsibility. Sometimes the confrontee attacks the confronter (verbally) to test whether the confronter will back down (typical aggressive behavior).

    Overshoot tactics are directed towards the confronter, with the intent of challenging the confronter.

Undershoot: There are many passive personalities at home, at work, and among friends. In the Undershoot, the confrontee becomes silent and non-responsive, or retreats into silence, a reflective state, or *self-pity*. In essence, the confrontee tries to evade his or her responsibility to resolve the Issue.

    Strategies used by the confrontee are not actually directed at the confronter, but rather *suppressed* and *internalized* by the confrontee. This behavior is more difficult to handle because the confrontee withdraws from communication, the very cornerstone of the confrontation technique.

Rule #23:   *Never back down. Always proceed. If troubled, Repeat the Fix or the C.C.S. That will give you time, and make the confrontee realize that you are serious.*

Components of the Overshoot:

Forgetting: The confrontee challenges the confronter by 'forgetting'—common *evasion* or *manipulation* attempts that can offer the confrontee an easy out: "Oh! I forgot …" It is an Overshoot because they are trying to get you to change. The best way to overcome this is to say: "That's another matter, which we will discuss later. But for now; what are you going to do about it?" (i.e., Repeat the Fix.)

Guilt: This is an attempt by the confrontee to *dump* responsibility onto the confronter. Be careful not to be caught by this trick. If it works, you're just about finished. Keep your mind and emotions clear. The best way to overcome this manipulation is to **ignore** the confrontee's comment. Let it slip right by you.

Example:

Who's Involved: Supervisor (you) and Employee (James)
Scenario: Operators in Plant #3 have been taking too many overtime hours. As the supervisor, you need to reduce overtime by five hours per operator.

You approach James, an operator, and present the issue. Immediately, James flares up. He looks straight at you and says, "You really don't like the way I work around here. As a matter of fact, you don't care much for me either!"

James gets emotional and challenges you personally. He attempts to make you remorseful of your alleged wrongdoings towards him. Should he succeed and convince you, then you must withdraw from confronting the issue of reducing overtime, at least with James.

Rule #24: *You do not have to respond to anything except the facts. If it is not factual, then proceed to your next fact (Facts #2 and #3) or repeat the Fix or C.C.S.*

Denial: This generally occurs when the confronter and the confrontee have previously discussed a matter or issue. Denial is a last-minute trick by the confrontee to avoid accountability — denying that the confronter ever mentioned the matter or issue. It attempts to put you into shock, i.e., break your concentration.

Rule #25: *Keep your facts up to date and well documented when discussing ongoing matters. Do not go into shock. State a supportive fact as to the time, place, and date. And repeat the Fix or C.C.S.*

Components of the Undershoot:

Withdrawal: The confrontee seeks inward silence and comfort from the issue presented by the confronter. The confrontee may attempt to go into several different inner worlds: self-pity, self-blame, low-self-esteem talk, crying, lying, or even pure silence. This technique is cumbersome. It may be necessary to reconvene at another time in order to let the confrontee become more relaxed, less intimidated, and better prepared to face you.

If the confronter is very aggressive, then chances are that he or she forces the confrontee to become more distant. Withdrawal is a reverse tactic by which the confrontee seeks not to cooperate. Hence, you've helped him to withdraw.

Rule #26: *Avoid shouting or screaming at a passive confrontee as an attempt to stimulate him (shouting is never recommended). Talk slowly, very clearly, and ask for a response. Use questions and ask for facts. Be polite and respectful.*

Escaping: An attempt by the confrontee to *rationalize* or *intellectualize* his way out of being accountable. Listen for statements like: "If I only had..." "The other guy doesn't have to do it; why do I?" "Hey! We've done it this way before," "That's not my job!" "Who needs a clean room, anyway?" These are attempts to escape accountability.

Rule #27: *Don't necessarily disagree with the rationalization or intellectualization. If they are true, then there's no reason for the Confrontee to further their escape. Stay focused on the issue. Repeat the Fix or the C.C.S. — that's the real and current Issue.*

Staying on the pyramid is the *responsibility* of the confronter and is essential. When the confrontee attempts to Overshoot or Undershoot, the confronter needs to heighten his awareness of the tactics used by the confrontee.

Obviously, the confrontee tries whatever works best for him. He may use all sorts of diversions (coughing, looking at someone else or things) or gaming techniques (jokes, flirting, intellectualizing). The Confrontation Model is designed to handle these tactics, and the confronter should stay firmly on the pyramid.

Rule #28: *Avoid all unnecessary conversations once on the pyramid.*

Eye-to-Eye and Emergency Stop

Figure 5-6 on the next page shows the components of the Eye-to-Eye and Emergency Stop.

Figure 5-6 Step-by-step explanation:

Eye-to-Eye: Here the confronter and the confrontee stand face-to-face, nose-to-nose, and eye-to-eye. This position ensures speaking the truth, concentrating, and eliminating most external noises or distractions. The more capable the confronter in focusing "eye-to-eye" on the confrontee, the better the chances are for a successful confrontation.

Rule #29: *Always look directly into the face of the Confronter. Never look away.*

Emergency Stop: One of the handiest tools for the confronter, the Emergency Stop is a safety measure. Use the "emergency stop" as you would a hand brake on an auto. Use it if you run out of facts, your confrontation deteriorates, or if the confrontee presents some good verifiable facts or evidence on his behalf and you need time to evaluate it.

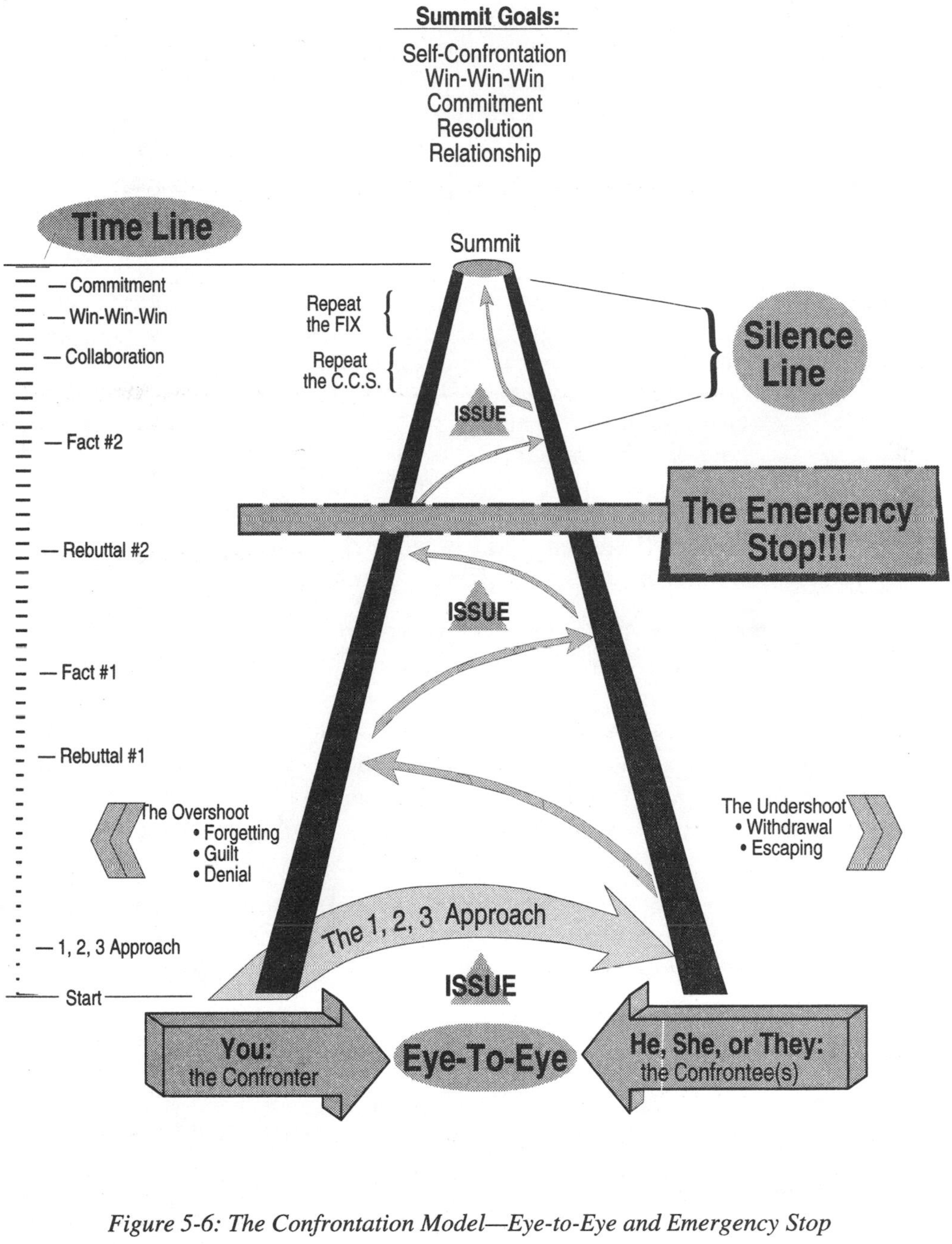

Summit Goals:

Self-Confrontation
Win-Win-Win
Commitment
Resolution
Relationship

Time Line

Summit

— Commitment

— Win-Win-Win

Repeat
the FIX

**Silence
Line**

— Collaboration

Repeat
the C.C.S.

ISSUE

— Fact #2

— Rebuttal #2

**The Emergency
Stop!!!**

ISSUE

— Fact #1

— Rebuttal #1

The Overshoot
• Forgetting
• Guilt
• Denial

The Undershoot
• Withdrawal
• Escaping

The 1, 2, 3 Approach

— 1, 2, 3 Approach

— Start

ISSUE

You:
the Confronter

Eye-To-Eye

He, She, or They:
the Confrontee(s)

Figure 5-6: The Confrontation Model—Eye-to-Eye and Emergency Stop

The *Emergency Stop* works like this. If, during a confrontation, the confronter needs to regroup or get more facts, he or she *temporarily stops* the confrontation dialogue. It is an official **postponement**. It is made clear that the confrontation will resume, but additional information is needed.

Rule #30:   ***When the Emergency Stop is invoked, always set a new time, date, and place to continue the confrontation.***

Rule #31:   ***Never apologize.***

Rule #32:   ***Return and continue the confrontation within 24 hours.***

Silence Line: The less the confronter talks the better. After several Facts and Rebuttals are exchanged, the confrontation dialogue moves toward the peak of the pyramid, where less room exists to move or change the direction of the dialogue. In many cases, providing the confronter keeps his or her big mouth shut, *the confrontee makes himself accountable*. Give him a chance to acknowledge his responsibility.

Rule #34:   ***Always remain silent after you present your facts, especially when you are near the top of the pyramid. After 15 seconds of dead silence, repeat the Fix or the C.C.S.***

Once you are actively on the pyramid, you're committed to guide the confrontation through the Win-Win-Win and into the Commitment. It's like a jet plane landing at an airport. Once the pilot is cleared to land, only an emergency can change the jet's course. The pilot is committed to land because the flight enters its most critical phase and is most vulnerable. The pilot must keep his eyes locked onto the runway and keep the plane in total control. He has a fixed amount of time before he lands the plane. And the more assured the pilot *feels* about the landing, the smoother the landing.

Likewise, the confronter must keep his eyes locked on the confrontee and stay focused. The confronter must be prepared, listen, and know how to properly work on the pyramid. There is a limited amount of time to get the facts out. Yes, you can use the Emergency Stop if you need to change the time and location of the confrontation. The more comfortable you *feel* with performing confrontations, the more skill you display. The more confidence you gain when handling problem situations, the greater your resolve to handle confrontations without fear.

Stand Firm

Figure 5-7 is about standing firm in your constant striving for Win-Win-Win and commitment. This is your driving motivation. Remember that your real purpose as a confronter is to coach the confrontee to creatively resolve the issue. Stand firm with

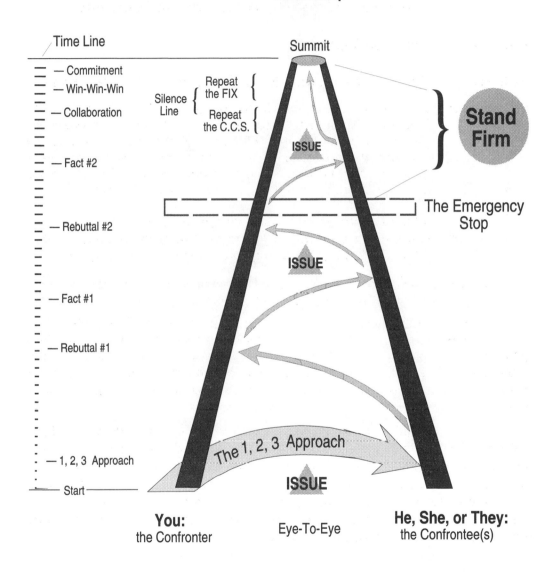

Figure 5-7: The Confrontation Model—Stand Firm

your focus and intent to improve the situation. The more confident you become when confronting, the easier it will be for the confrontee to succeed as well. Figure 5-7 shows the elements of the Stand Firm strategy.

Figure 5-7 Step-by-step explanation:

Stand Firm: Always maintain confidence and integrity in what you say. Do not deviate. Do not yield. Make every effort possible to enable the confrontee to create a *winning solution*.

Recall the Communication Model. What is the most important element of the sender? Think about its application in the Confrontation Model. The answer is the element of Intent.

Rule #34:   ***The Confronter's intention must be to reach a Win-Win-Win outcome.***

Win-Win-Win: There need not be any losers. The confronter's Intent motivates the confrontee to a positive, winning situation. This also strengthens the relationship, so that it, too, is a winner.

Rule #35:   ***The more sincere the Intent, the stronger the subliminal message of your sincerity will be. This encourages the confrontee to seek a Win-Win-Win Resolution.***

Commitment: The confrontee must convince you that he or she can successfully resolve the issue. His or her statement must demonstrate strong and unquestionable conviction. Commitment is what carries the confrontation scenario dialogue to its resolution or completion. Asking for commitment empowers the confronter and sets the path for building a closer relationship or at least, respect between the confronter and confrontee. It also empowers the confrontee to stay focused on his or her obligation to creatively and intuitively resolve the issue.

"Gut-level" commitment: One of the greatest tools you now posses is your gut level sensation. Gut-level feelings can give you instant feedback: favorable and those of caution. Whenever a confrontee commits to a change, he or she will, in most cases, initiate a reaction located in your belly.

These gut-level feelings actually let you know if and how serious the confrontee's commitment was. We need to become more familiar with our gut-level sensations and learn how to depend on them. We've all had gut-level feelings before, but may not realized how important they are and what messages they bring.

Commitment

The dictionary definition of *commitment* is "a pledge to carry out a particular course of action, backed up with an emotional and/or intellectual binding." This is what the confronter expects from the confrontee, and the confrontee must not only make such a pledge, but be fully prepared to back it up with the necessary change in behavior, action, attitude, belief, or whatever is needed.

Rule #36:   *The confronter must sense the Confrontee's Commitment.*
The confrontee must express it in a manner that shows it
comes from the heart.

The confronter can also make a commitment. This technique is called a "**double-barrel commitment.**" It is an excellent strategy at this stage for the confronter to make a commitment. "I can commit to this…" based on the completion of the Resolution. Or, should the Resolution be breached, "I can commit to the action of …"

When the confrontee hears the confronter making a statement of commitment, he or she may perceive a sense of solidarity or possibly a warning. Therefore, the confronter should recognize the importance of this strategy and be prepared to make a commitment also.

A final comment on commitment: a friend shared with me the following passage:

> *Commitment is what transforms a promise into a reality.*
> *It is the words that speak boldly of your intentions;*
>   *and the actions which speak louder than words.*
> *It is making time when there is none;*
>   *coming through time after time, year after year.*
> *Commitment is the stuff character is made of;*
>   *the power to change the face of things.*
> *It is the daily triumph of integrity over skepticism.*
>   *– Anonymous*

Resolution

Resolution is "a course of action determined and adopted, backed by a formal statement of the decision." The confrontee now moves to deliver whatever behavior, action, or change is needed to bring about the desired outcome.

Resolution: The purpose of confronting is to respectfully resolve issues, correct problems, and "get the show on the road."

Once you obtain the confrontee's commitment, move on to *resolution*. The following guidelines will make the resolution process more workable and successful:

- In order for the confrontee to assume ownership and accountability, get him or her to recommend and design the resolution. The confronter should avoid dominating this phase unless absolutely necessary
- Collaboration is fine, but resolution ownership must remain with the confrontee, unless the situation dictates otherwise
- Affirm the criteria needed in the resolution, i.e., what are the important things that need to be done
- Set a time and date for completion of the resolution. Resolution need not occur during the confrontation dialogue, but some time in the immediate or near future.

Rule #37: *The Confrontation process is not complete until Resolution is acknowledged by the confronter.*

The confronter *must* immediately attend to an unsatisfactorily completed resolution. When a confrontee falls short of his or her commitment or reneges on the proper completion of a resolution, a *new issue* has been generated—*breach of commitment*. This is very serious for now the relationship is truly in jeopardy. The confronter now has two issues to confront: the initial issue and the breach issue. When the confrontee breaches, the supposedly Win-Win-Win looks more like lose-lose-lose.

Dealing with the breach issue empowers the confronter to create a resolution which may serve to separate the confrontee from the relationship. The confronter may position the outcome of the confrontation to reflect a win-lose-lose outcome whereby the confrontee "loses" in order for the resolution to be accomplished at the expense of the confrontee's extradition from the relationship.

For example, a supervisor confronts an employee a third time for tardiness. During the confrontation, the employee commits not to be late anymore, and the supervisor commits to automatically suspend the employee for a week if he should renege on this resolution. The employee agrees, so when the employee is late, the supervisor informs him that he has already approved the resulting action, and suspension is immediate and automatic. This process greatly reduces stress on the supervisor because accountability has been predetermined: the employee owns the pain, not the supervisor. This major "stress" eliminating technique is a very valuable asset.

Completing the Confrontation

Do not rehash the confrontation with the confrontee. Honor his or her space to feel and then reflect on the confrontation dialogue just completed. Also, keep in mind that the quicker you arrive at a Win-Win-Win situation, the more respect you gain, and the less lost time accrues.

Rule #38:   ***Separate from the Confrontee immediately after the Commitment. It is better not to discuss the Confrontation with the Confrontee. At that time, you are presenting a personal empowerment skill. You are showing decision-making and leadership abilities. Do not dilute it by rehashing it with the confrontee.***

Attention

Another conerstone of the Confrontation Model is **attention**. An important survival technique of the Samurai warrior was total, unrelenting attention in every momet! By attention, we mean: *the elimination of any thought which is not directly related to the subject or issue of the confrontation.*

For example, just prior to the confrontation, do not think about calling your spouse on the phone about paying the bills. And do not allow interruptions or incoming calls during the process. Effective confrontation requires a great deal of mental energy. Give it your all, because it is a serious undertaking.

How well have you defined the issue? How well do you know the facts and their implications? You must be able to probe deeper and deeper. *The more you perceive, the more you can know*. This skill is called **concentration**. The more you concentrate, i.e., focus, the more you understand what is taking place.

Rule #39:   ***The person who confronts must concentrate on the Issue at all times.***

Preparation

There are two different types of events in the process of confronting:

Planning Event: Before you approach another person or group in the process of confronting, you must plan out the event as best as possible. By planning, we mean **get the facts**—all of them—and define a strategy. Remember, a successful confrontation leads the confrontee to a Win-Win-Win situation. And don't forget, getting Commitment and Resolution from the confrontee!

Spontaneous Event (on-the-spot): How do you confront a person who suddenly, out of nowhere, confronts you? An issue arises and someone else initiates a confrontation with you. The most strategic action you can take is to clarify the Issue.

Rule #40:   ***Do not proceed with a spontaneous confrontation until you have clarified the Issue.***

Clarification is only possible when you give it your full *attention*. Once you have done this, take the lead in the conversation, get into the 1–2–3 Approach, and begin the confrontation. (Note: More detail on Spontaneous Confrontations is presented in a later chapter.)

❑ **Hint:** **To aid you during a confrontation, envision an illuminated Confrontation Model sitting on top of the confrontee's right shoulder. As you move up the Model, an invisible light bean tracks your progress and reminds you of your focus.**

Conclusion

Review and make sure that you comfortably understand the **entire** Confrontation Model— its concept, structure, elements, terms, and techniques. Bear in mind that the Confrontation Model is a life-long learning tool. Psychologically speaking, it is a behaviorally learned process which becomes habit-forming, that is, automatic. It has power. The more you apply it, the easier it becomes to confront issues and difficult people. The more you use it, the more you confront things spontaneously. The more that happens, the less you have on your mind to deal with and the more time you have to enjoy the person you really are.

Are you finished *scripting*? At this point, you need to ascertain that you have replaced or "de-programmed" all your old scripts. If you feel that more practice is worthwhile, then practice and start applying these techniques. This will undoubtedly assist with your scripting.

Guidelines for Role-playing the Confrontee

Practice drills will require the assistance of a friend, family member or co-worker to role-play the confrontee. Instruct them to say whatever comes to his or her mind. The following guidelines will also help the confrontee to be a better role-player and serve your needs:

1. These exercises are intended to assist the confronter to strengthen his or her confidence and consistency while applying the techniques of the Confrontation Model

2. Your function is to help the confronter to practice—avoid discouraging remarks and dialogues

3. Stay focused on the contents of the issue or scenario

4. Avoid shutting down the confronter. Feed realistic Rebuttals from which the confronter can stay in control and focused.

5. Be serious and supportive of the confronter's desire to practice properly and successfully

6. Try different approaches, e.g., passive–aggressive, or Overshoot and Undershoot tactics.

7. Use the Appendices for practice scenarios

8. Critique the confronter after he or she completes the Confrontation Model process

9. Switch roles a few times to get a well-rounded perspective

10. Encourage the confronter to practice until he or she feels comfortable and shows consistency

11. Do a Warm-up Scenario in Appendix B for practice. If you use audio-video equipment, make sure you zoom in on your face.

12. Be honest with yoursel, if not, confront yourself.

The Secrets of Nonverbal Communication

Let's face it! We've all flirted at least once in our lifetime. Recall how you felt —a little excited, maybe embarrassed, infatuated. Remember your thoughts about how it could be with that special person. Flirtations and accompanying expressions are *nonverbal communication*. Imagine the feelings that occurred when that other person offered a return compliment. Wow!

Another good example to which we can all relate took place in elementary school. Remember when the teacher walked around the room and asked us questions? Didn't the teacher probe our faces to see who was faking and trying to avoid getting called. Guess who got called?

The eyes, the mouth, the tilt of the head relate thoughts and messages. A person who covers his mouth with his hand offers us clues to his character, possibly his insecurities, or that he has bad breath. This chapter intends to surface some of the secrets of *nonverbal detection* — a process that enables the confronter to better grasp the many facets of nonverbal communication.

Comment: **The difference between nonverbal communication and nonverbal detection is that detection is a process of observing a person (or yourself, for that matter) moving into and or out of bodily positions and facial expressions.**

The scope of this chapter discusses both the *sender* and the *receiver*. It focuses on how to **detect** nonverbal communication which primarily comes from the upper portion of the body. Investigation of nonverbal activities such as:

- Body movement
- Voice inflection (pitch and tone)
- Facial expression

These provides us with a wealth of information. We also delve into a few of the finer nonverbal characteristics that may help us detect which of the three *Confrontation Behavioral Types* we are confronting.

Comment: **The unspoken word is often seen.**

The best place to start with nonverbal detection is *you*, because to know more about yourself also provides a greater understanding of others.

The Sender (You)

For the purposes of this chapter, consider yourself to be the sender and the confronter with regard to both Models. You need to take inventory of the way you appear to others. The following exercise is an excellent tool.

❑ Mirror Exercise

Stand in front of a mirror. (Note: A video camera and playback monitor replace the mirror in training workshops.)

The first process puts you in touch with your eyes and also helps you understand the other people's perception of you. Remember, good communication requires sincere eye contact. Look straight into your eyes for five minutes. (If you wear glasses, take them off for this exercise. Focus directly into the mirror, straight into your eyes. Do this for at least five minutes. Put your glasses back on, and place the mirror about 12 to 18 inches away from your face. Again, look straight into your face for at least five minutes.)

Observe your face as a variety of thoughts and emotions flow through you. Next, answer the following questions:

- Do my eyes talk back to me?
- Does my nose look different?
- Do I have good laugh lines?
- Is my facial expression sincere?
- Does wearing glasses distract others from seeing the true me?
- Do I tend to tilt my head?
- Do I feel confident about my smile?
- Does the way I comb my hair reflect my energy and personality?
- Do I like looking at myself?
- Does my face reflect honesty and integrity?
- When others look at my face, will they see the real me?
- Can others enjoy my smile?
- Can others sense my thoughts by reading my facial expressions?
- Does my face express serious thought and concern when deliberating?
- Do I look straight forward, or tend to look up or down slightly?
- Do I look slightly to the side? If so, which side do I favor?
- Do I feel good about talking to myself through a mirror?

Your most honest answers serve two extremely important purposes:

(a) Feedback on how you perceive yourself and how others will see you as a confronter. Rarely does any person or friend offer you this kind of personal feedback to enhance your nonverbal communication skills.

(b) Gives you a better interpretation of the nonverbal communication cues of others. The above questions serve to guide and familiarize you when identifying nonverbal messages. They enhance your level of awareness of the other person's nonverbal actions. The questions can be used as a **Detector Check List**, which may help you perceive bodily expressions of others during conversation.

Suppose during a confrontation dialogue, you are near the top of the pyramid model. You notice that the confrontee's face becomes taut, loses color, and he is staring off to the side. The question: "Does my face display serious thought and concern when silently deliberating?" tells you that the confrontee is either taking the time to create a solution, or is just pondering and waiting for your direction.

At this point, it is important that you maintain control. You may respond: "Well, John, do we have your cooperation?" That statement kindles movement on the pyramid. It calls the *issue* into focus, and shows the confrontee that you are in control and aware of his deliberating, while eliciting a decision on his part.

If, instead, you see John looking downward (possibly an Undershoot), you may interpret his nonverbal message as guilt or shame, and respond: "John, you're not the issue, so let's stay objective. How do you propose to correct the problem?"

In this case, John's nonverbal message clued you in on his hesitation: embarrassment or emotional condition. He needed direction and some motivation to help guide him to a Win-Win-Win situation.

Nonverbal detection requires careful consideration, interpretation, and skill. In the example above, we made conjectures — we didn't have all the facts. However, we should be cautious and observe two rules with regard to nonverbal interpretation:

Rule #41:   *Avoid prejudging. Don't act in haste. Don't assume your interpretation of nonverbals is always 100% accurate.*

Rule #42:   *Ask probing questions to clarify your interpretations. Act calm ly and sincerely. Instill confidence in the confrontee that you understand his or her situation.*

Your Body Language

As the sender or confronter, your body language transmits your emotional state (excitement, sincerity, commitment) toward the issue. Chances are that you would not buy a TV from a salesperson who showed no enthusiasm about the quality and operation of the set. If the body language of the confronter does not signal active engagement in the process, the confrontee will probably not "buy into" it either.

When confronting others:

- Speak up clearly
- Position your body about **three to five** feet in front of the other person*
- Keep your chin level
- Keep your shoulders squared
- Stand upright
- Look directly at the face of the other person**
- Let your hands tend somehow to find their own natural movement and place; avoid the common arms across the chest *(cut-off)* and the arms behind the back *(power)* postures.
- In addition, avoid forcing hand movements, though, try to use them to express yourself. Don't be rigid, and whatever you do, don't droop or act like a wimp. Women, in particular, get turned off by men who portray a "wimpish" character or position—it's a deadly posture in the business setting***

(Notes:

*   The need for personal space depends on the culture. For example, it is greater for Japanese and northern European cultures, and less for southern Europe.

**   Some cultures will find this threatening or even combative.

*** The Japanese find sudden hand and arm movements threatening)

Facial expressions provide additional nonverbal signals. Use your eyes, but do not stare. Staring can mesmerize you, distract others, and sever your control of the conversation. Establish good *eye contact,* move your head occasionally to the side, up or down, and always maintain strong eye contact. Watch the newscasters on the evening news — they are coached in that technique. Good eye contact and slight movements of your face and body keep attention levels high for both you and the other person.

Voice inflection serves to *pull-in* or *push-out* the distance between sender and receiver. Yell at somebody and he tends to move back. Talk harshly or sharply to a person and you shut him down. On the other hand, if you talk extremely softly, other people tend to come closer, but if they sense no urgency, they will withdraw. Speak consistently and clearly. Practice speaking aloud to your favorite friend in the mirror.

The Receiver (The Other Person)

As the receiver talks, the sender has the opportunity to *hear* keenly what the receiver says and can also *see* nonverbals emanating from the receiver. This attention to the other's verbal and nonverbal communication is part of *Active Listening.*

❏ Did you know?

The average person speaks about 125 words per minute and can listen to approximately 400 words per minute. The difference is 275 words per minute. This offers the listener an opportunity to actively listen and read between the lines—the nonverbals. Therefore, when one person is speaking, the other is able to listen carefully, detect nonverbal communication, and feel the other out for commitment, sincerity, honesty, integrity, etc.

There are many good books on body language, but most of your answers will come from good eye contact that produces unique insight into a person's *level of integrity*. Once the basis of integrity has been established, the relationship matures. You can progress rapidly as a communicator and a confronter based on trust, the foundation of True Understanding.

Beyond words, *nonverbal detection* helps identify how truthful other people are in their interaction with you. When people communicate with you, their body "radiates" their energy. If the body appears to heighten and energize, and lean slightly forward, then this reveals to you that there may be truth and conviction behind the words. On the other hand, should the body lean back, or seem lifeless or hesitant, then be cautious and probe the receiver's responses. During a dialogue, a person who believes that his response is truthful wants you to accept it. After he completes a statement, he may look directly at you and say: "Do you follow me …?" attempting to secure a True Understanding.

If *doubt* or *hesitation* are exhibited, you probably will hear something like: "Well, … er … there are many things that I must consider, though, I am somewhat conservative on the issue (a nonsense statement, without a True Understanding)." Notice also that he might even attempt to act sophisticated by looking at you, but he will soon turn around and come back to you, timidly asking, "Do you see my point of view?"

Be careful when people cannot stand firm on what they say, especially if their attempts to state a True Understanding fail. Look carefully at their body language; it tends to leave you feeling empty. *Standing* or *sitting* within five feet or less helps you "sense" the other person's level of energy and comfort, especially when both of you are sitting.

Rule #43: *Make every effort to stand when confronting. Try to stand between 3 and 5 feet apart.*

Sitting tends to reduce the effectiveness of the confrontation, however, it does serve to make both parties more comfortable and less threatened. Sitting is also good with *passive* Confrontation Behavior Types.

Leaning forward implies interest, heightened listening, acceptance. Leaning backward implies disinterest and lack of involvement. A confronter may need to invoke the Fix again to get the confrontee to own the issue.

Eyes, nose, mouth, chin

Let us look at the facial relationship of the eyes, nose, mouth, and chin. How many people have you witnessed speaking with their chin resting on their upper chest, their nose blocking the mouth, and the eyes zigzagging slowly while looking at your feet? A salesman would starve to death with those talents.

What would this mean to you? Outright lies, guilt or shame, or sincere incompetence? Children are great at such evasive maneuvers, and you, the parent, must rely on past behaviors exhibited by the child. A good response with an adult would be, "George, talk up a little because I need to listen carefully to what you have to say." This informs the receiver (George), that you are not convinced at this point with his reply to you. Also, a True Understanding has not yet been conveyed and he needs to try again. In most cases, remain cautious of verbal communication until the nonverbal communication satisfies you. You can feel it!

In the opposite combination, the eyes, nose, mouth, and chin are *too high* and somewhat *snobbish.* All too often, the receiver looks down your throat while you look up his nostrils. This tends to force something by you. Back-off a step or two and say, "George, run that by me again."

He has to rethink the approach and that causes him to either get mad or hesitate. This signals for you to watch-out: something isn't honest nor complete, and the receiver labels himself as a suspicious communicator.

Twitching of the mouth signals another nervous habit, just as excessive *laughing.* When that happens, slow the conversation down and verify the True Understanding.

Hand Movements

The receiver's *hands* tell us a lot, too. *Closed fists* and *pointing* signal aggressive thoughts and behavior. Raised fists display power similar to the overkill handshake. Hands which constantly stay rigidly at a person's side usually reflect lack of excitement just as the "wimpy" handshake: the ones which feel like you just touched an uncooked knockwurst.

Hand movements express *creativity* and generally complement the verbal messages. *Palms* facing up may signal a giving or humbling nonverbal message. The typical *crossed arms* can mean several different things. Be very careful that you look at the face and the entire body before concluding what that body posture is conveying. Usually, a person standing flat-footed and *erect with crossed arms* displays a stand-off defensive position. When the arms are crossed, though lower and more relaxed, and the person leans to one side, it connotes a comfortable listening mode.

Italians are noted for excessive hand movements. If you are not familiar with cultural mannerisms, then don't prejudge the behavior.

Some people cover their mouths with their hands when speaking, indicating either the need for major dental work, or insecurity around people.

Nervous and *fidgeting* hands can indicate a preoccupied mind or that a person is not concentrating on the subject discussed. *Head scratching, jingling change* in the pocket, or *pulling the ear* may be a nervous habit that tells you that the person has trouble with responding a True Understanding.

Nonverbal Characteristics for Each Confrontation Behavior Type

Aggressive, passive, and assertive behaviors provide you with valuable nonverbal clues which help you better understand the individual's behavior during the confrontation process.

Aggressive: A most *unfavorable* behavior. Aggressive confrontation behavior is dominant, commonly resulting in a put-down of the other person. He tends to *choose for others,* rather than let them choose for themselves. An aggressive person *invades* other people's space, making them feel defensive and often humiliated. Although the aggressive person seeks to impose his point of view in the confrontation, he does not appropriately express his feelings, which later may result in guilt.

Your approach: Don't counter-attack! You may initially agree, but don't accept his response (unless it's correct); ask for more insight and understanding. Ask him to repeat his answer or statement. Don't get emotional, defensive or withdraw. Hold your ground and *ask questions*. Stay within the focus lines of the Confrontation Model. Ask for his reply. The more you get him to talk and state the facts, the less aggressive he acts and the more balance between you and he exists.

Passive: A passive person allows others to choose for him in order to *avoid conflict*. The result of this action often is the lack of achievement of desired goals. During the confrontation, their main objective is to shut down and make you frustrated—that's a tactic! This behavior usually generates feelings of self-denial, anxiety, and resentment. The passive behavior denies a person from expressing his or her true feelings. It ignores personal rights of the individual acting passive, as well as others who want to collaborate. On the other hand, passive behavior tempts others to infringe on those rights. The effect on others is that they may feel either guilty or superior.

Your approach: Confront with respect. Avoid talking "down" to them. Keep positive and offer genuine *excitement*. Maintain good *eye contact* and sincere nonverbals. Avoid aggressive communication behavior. Speak one-to-one or privately rather than with others around or in groups. Recommend that you both *sit down*. **Listen carefully** and let the passive person assume the lead. Agree when possible and offer encouragement often. Ask for recommendations. Stir a little creativity in their minds—they'll respect you for it.

Assertive: A person who practices assertiveness expresses his or her feelings openly and honestly in such a way that the rights of others are not infringed upon. The assertive person acts out his own needs and desires, *without denying others* their own needs and feelings. Assertive confrontation behavior's effect on you is displayed in *confidence* and *self-respect*.

Your approach: Encourage this type of confrontation behavior. When interacting with another assertive communicator, converse in your usual assertive manner—be yourself! Consistent assertive confrontations are excellent role-model tactics for parents, managers, and interactive people. Assertive behavior is admired and emulated.

When confronting with *aggressive* or *passive* communicators, try the following:

1. Maintain your assertiveness; avoid becoming passive or aggressive yourself
2. Move back a step or two when conversing with an aggressive confronter; avoid the temptation of feeding comments into his aggressive role; make sure your nonverbals communicate confidence to the other person
3. Be patient, factual, sincere, and try to create a True Understanding for each communication cycle.

In summary, nonverbal communications are body movements as well as subliminal "unspoken" words which complement the spoken words. It is the language of the body that enhances a person's ability to effectively confront. It serves to ensure that a True Understanding was conveyed, and that the journey to the top of the pyramid is accomplished.

Nonverbal detection is an open-ended learning experience. There are thousands of applications and variations to learn and confidently apply. The individual who seeks to improve his or her skills in detecting and interpreting nonverbals must conscientiously strive to seek opportunities as a communicator and confronter.

The Psychology of Confronting

The essence of personal growth encompasses the human triad of body, mind, and spirit. Developmentally, that is, speaking psychologically, many activities of confrontation are involved in each of these three aspects of the human. We will briefly explore the phenomena which surround them. Should the following interest you, then there are plenty of resources available for further reading.

Confrontation and the Three Egos

Many people are in awe as they observe a newborn child — the little spiritual thing! But what's not observed is the infant's "body intelligence," or **body-ego**. It knows what it needs. Parents soon find that out.

As the infant develops, he or she confronts many challenges and spontaneously seeks to resolve them — a natural process, indeed. From childhood to adulthood, the body intelligence dwindles because of the **mental ego's** surging dominance. This imbalance is like a Lose-Win situation. For the suppressed body-ego to survive, it must stand firm by understanding its emotions and by expressing its feelings. This aspect of confrontation is what is lacking in so many of us. It's also labeled "low self-esteem" or even "lack of confidence."

How do the body-ego and mental-ego learn to cooperate? Psychologically, there are many ways: the Confrontation Model is one. The searching and humbling mental-ego confronts embedded suppressions and obstacles — *this is the primary aspect of self-confrontation*. The body-ego, in turn, surrenders its hold on the embedded suppressions and impasses as well. The cooperative effect upon the individual is truly a *healing process*. Therefore, as we learn the art of confronting others, we invariably learn how to confront ourselves. One might ask: "Who needs a therapist?"

The **spiritual-ego**, which has a primary role of *server*, becomes activated when the body- and mental-egos are cooperating, and *truly integrated*. Individuals who experience this feel a surge of *life* and *happiness* through them. Confronting ourselves and others simply becomes a matter of routine. Our lives radiate with self-esteem and confidence. Above all, we can trust ourselves in any situation.

It should be noted that as we begin to trust ourselves, instinctively and intuitively, the more we trust our feelings and express the "real" you. This simplifies our decision-making process and ability to confront issues. This process becomes more efficient, needless to say, the more charismatic you will feel.

When others bear witness to your spiritual-healing charisma:

1. People respect you and enjoy your company
2. People tend not to bother confronting you with their problems or short-comings, i.e., they tend to leave you alone.
3. People feel happy around you.

Application

To master the Confrontation Model, read Chapters 4 – 6 several times. Understand and memorize both models. Master the ability to *self-detect* your own areas of weakness when using these models. For instance, if you have trouble focussing while communicating, then there exists a chance that your *Intent* was not strong enough. Thus, you were restrained and your cycle of communication began to weaken. By knowing the models and all their primary components, you can pinpoint techniques or behaviors which you may need to improve. *You teach yourself!*

Work on the Communication Model first. Practice it until you've gotten it down pat! Apply it consistently by visualizing the model in your mind as much as possible during each conversation. Once you become accomplished with that, begin to work on the Confrontation Model in the same manner. Start with the "Warm-up" and "Easy" scenarios in Appendices B and C. You may want to use a mirror for practice (Chapter 5). Also important: play out the role of the confrontee in order to get another perspective of the interaction.

Another proven way to be a better confronter is to share the experience of learning it with your spouse, a close friend, or your teenage child. Try different aspects of the Confrontation Model. For instance, how are you applying the 1–2–3 Approach? Are you comfortable with formulating the Clear Concise Statement (C.C.S.) which takes some effort and a little creativity. Presenting an issue in eight words or less is an art-form and needs to become second nature.

Stating the Fix in the early stages of learning the Confrontation Model is difficult for many people. Once they find that the process is advantageous, they routinely execute the step. However, we have had students of the Confrontation Skills Training over-emphasize the Fix once they saw the power in it.

Asking for Commitment is quite unusual for most people. When was the last time you heard someone ask you for commitment? "Practice makes perfect" as you so often heard. Getting the confrontee to give you a "gut level" *commitment* is a major step in changing his or her behavior.

Practice, Practice, Practice! — the bottom-line. Each time you exercise with the Confrontation Model, be open-minded and critique yourself. Learn and become more successful as a confronter. Your life will become clearer, you will be healthier, your mind more peaceful, and you will enjoy more freedom. You are becoming psychologically strong because you are finally expressing your true and higher self!

Advanced Confrontation Techniques

We dedicate this chapter to expanding your skill, and exploring variants of the Confrontation Model. In addition, we will present ways to help you personalize some of the Confrontation Model's techniques to suit your psychological and behavioral styles.

This chapter discusses three major advanced areas in detail:

- Multiple Issues
- Spontaneous Confrontations
- Super-Negative Confrontee

Multiple Issues

Multiple issues can occur during a confrontation. As a result of the dialogue, you may detect other pending issues. You must decide if the new *issue*:

a) is a more important *issue* than the initial *issue* and needs to be addressed immediately.

b) is secondary to the initial *issue* and should be addressed afterwards.

The primary rule in confrontation is concentrate on the *issue*! If you try to concentrate on two issues, you're bound to confuse them. Once you detect the existence of multiple issues, two major rules apply:

Rule #44: **Given multiple issues, confront the most important *issue* first.**

Rule #45: **Separate each *issue* and give each *issue* its own pyramid.**

Whenever confronting, always remember that each *issue* has its own pyramid. It takes a very skilled person to keep thoughts and rationale in focus for two or three pyramids. Best to stay with the most important *issue* and return to the secondary *issue(s)* afterwards.

In many cases, the confrontee tries to introduce another *issue* or issues to distract you. You must listen carefully and quickly ask yourself: Is it a distraction or a valid *issue*?

Keep the initial *issue* in focus unless presented with facts or evidence of another, more important *issue*. If it is a valid *issue* and is more important than the existing *issue*, then and only then do you postpone the initial *issue*.

Once confident that the newly surfaced *issue* is in fact secondary, proceed with the original confrontation. It makes the confrontee understand your discipline and determination to reach a Win-Win-Win situation.

In this case, proceed normally up the pyramid. Make it clear that you will further investigate the other *issue(s)* and that you will provide feedback.

With regards to the new *issue*, should confrontation take place now or later? This depends on whether or not you want a clear-cut Win-Win-Win outcome. You'll need to ask yourself a few questions:

1. Do you have enough facts to guide you through the new confrontation?
2. Do you know exactly where you want to direct this new confrontation?
3. Are you confident that you understand the new *issue*?
4. Do you have total control of the confrontation interaction, i.e., are you properly climbing the pyramid?

If you can answer "yes" to all the above questions, then you can evoke the Emergency Stop for the initial *issue* (See Figure 5.6) and begin a new Confrontation Pyramid with a new 1–2–3 Approach.

Rule #46: **Seek a Win-Win-Win orientation. The closer you get to the truth of any issue, the greater the Commitment – the greater the Resolve!**

The greater the resolve, the higher the probability that a situation will change, such as when a person resolves to lose weight. The degree of success depends largely on the resolve to succeed. Resolve can be your decision to:

1. Use firmness of purpose
2. Strive for a formal resolution
3. Engage determination
4. Make a firm decision
5. Wake up and live.

Rule #47: **Always attempt to collaborate upwards on the pyramid. Ask for the facts. Encourage the confrontee to contribute to the Win-Win-Win situation.**

If you have any doubt or feel hesitant, then postpone a new confrontation. Maintain control and know the objective you want to reach with the confrontee. In this case, your choice is twofold:

1. Invoke the Emergency Stop and set a new time and date to continue with the confrontation, or
2. Continue with the current *issue* with the understanding that you'll investigate the other *issue* and provide feedback within the shortest time possible.

Spontaneous Confrontations

Spontaneous Confrontations are based on impromptu situations. These situations demand from us a sense of alertness and skill. Experience tells us that being caught off guard only makes things more difficult for us. So be prepared.

Rule #48: **The moment someone confronts you (spontaneously), you become the receiver of the conversation — the confrontee.**

Rule #49: **If caught in a spontaneous confrontation, you must become the Sender—the Confronter—as quickly as possible.**

Rule #50: **Your Intent: Find out the *issue*.**

(Note: Refer to "Intent" on Figure 4-3: Core Elements of the Communication Model)

When confronted by another person, become the confronter. If the person confronting you possesses poor confrontation skills, your leadership role will most likely serve as a benefit to him or her. Some key points to remember are:

- Quickly divorce yourself from all other activities and objectives.
- Listen carefully. Ask for clarification. If necessary, repeat the person's statement.
- Seek out the *issue*.
- Clarify the *issue*.
- Get acknowledgment that you understand the *issue*
- Gain composure, regroup your thoughts, and picture the Confrontation Model's pyramid in your mind.
- Seek agreement on the *issue*.
- Take charge!—become the confronter
- Immediately use the 1–2–3 Approach.
- Begin working upwards on the pyramid.

The next scenario provides an example of a spontaneous confrontation:

Who's Involved: Supervisor and Mechanic
Scenario: You, the supervisor, are walking through the work area. Mike, the maintenance mechanic, impolitely stops you. You're instantly taken off guard. Then Mike says: "Thank's a lot. You never got back to me with the information I needed."

At this point, you are the receiver and the confrontee. Your response is critical. You must concentrate. Mike is mad because he needs some feedback you were supposed to give him. Is the *issue*:

    (a)   You're not getting back with Mike? or

    (b)   The information needed by Mike?

By your calm and confident statements and directives, you give Mike a chance to cool off. You also give yourself a moment or two to recall the information. If you know the information, *give it to him quickly*. But don't get aroused. If you can't remember, ask him to refresh your memory. You must assume the lead in the conversation. Look at him squarely in the eye, with sincerity and confidence, say: "Mike... pause ... is the *issue* my not getting back with you?"

Other responses could include:

> "Shucks! You're right!"
> "Thanks for reminding me."
> "I'm glad you came to me."
> "Mike, forgive me..."
> "If I do this again, I'll buy the coffee."
> "Mike, please clue me in..."
> "Just be a little more specific, Mike."

Guidelines to remember

- Don't panic.
- Keep cool. Restrain your emotions.
- Let the other person speak. The more he or she talks, the more time you have to think.
- If you don't have any input, say so! Better to tell the truth rather than give misleading facts.
- If the confrontation seems to drag on, then invoke the Emergency Stop. Get back with the other person as soon as you get the facts.

Hostile Confronter

At some point, you may encounter a "hostile." If so, take the offensive. Prepare for the hostile's strategy, but avoid prejudging. Be cautious and alert. This is best facilitated by insisting on factual information and by all means, keep the conversation short!

Let's learn a few traits of super-negative people. The list to follow delineates many of the more obvious traits and characteristics of a hostile. Copy the list below onto a separate sheet of paper, right the name of an individual whom you would classify as hostile, but please don't be judgmental! You're only being observant and want to learn. Observe to see how many items on the list which the super-negative person actually demonstrates. This exercise will help you learn more about the Performance Behaviors listed in Figure 5.1.

- Face usually look mad, angered, troubled.
- Rarely looks up.
- Speaks forcibly loud.

- Has hundreds of negative things to say.
- Not friendly or offering compliments.
- Out to share negativity and make you unhappy.
- Always wants to win at others expense
- Has few, if any, valid facts.
- Don't care if your feelings are hurt. As a matter of fact, takes pride in that process.
- Interrupts you.
- Creates distractions and irrelevancies to throw you off.
- Not outwardly creative.
- Usually focused on the past and negatively on the future.
- Incessant complaints, but few solutions.
- Doesn't like to listen.
- May be very lazy.
- Is impatient and wants immediate solutions.

Now that you have a better understanding of these fine folks, we can discuss how to better interact with them during a confrontation.

Rule #51:   Avoid spontaneous confrontations with hostiles. Set the confrontation up carefully.

Hostiles involved in spontaneous confrontations usually display hot tempers, become either very emotional or cold, and may act frustrated. Generally, it is not the ideal setting for a Win-Win-Win outcome. Hostiles usually make an effort to keep you from winning, and use you and the situation as a platform for their "performance."

If confronted by a hostile, take the following steps:

- Listen.
- Don't talk.
- Take a deep breath; count to five.
- Show concern before you say anything.
- Take the time to prepare yourself. You think faster than he speaks. He is also cooling down.
- Repeat his statement for clarity of the *issue*.
- Take charge. Picture the pyramid.
- Determine the *issue*.
- Reverse the confrontation—you confront rather than he.
- Use the 1–2–3 Approach

During the confrontation, obey the following rules:

Rule #52:   Never get emotional with hostiles

Rule #53:   **Be concise and precise: always factual**

Rule #54:   **Never get off on tangents – stay on the issue**

Rule #55:   **Talk slowly, firmly, clearly, and with confidence!**

Rule #56:   **Repeat the 1–2–3 Approach, i.e., the C.C.S. or the FIX, as often as necessary.**

Rule #57:   **Do not ever speak immediately after *YOU* asked a question or demanded an answer. Stay totally silent, even for a minute, if necessary.**

Rule #58:   **Always look the hostile in the face, and maintain eye contact.**

Rule #59:   **Invoke the Emergency Stop if the hostile gets out of hand; but never permit the confrontation to go permanently unresolved.**

The key to winning with hostiles is to demonstrate persistent confidence in yourself. Over time, they will know exactly who they are bargaining with, and will be less negative, at least to you! The general rule is that the more powerful and confident you are, the less they will bother you.

Personalizing the Confrontation Model

It is obvious by now to realize that to be a successful confronter you must personalize it. The whole essence of proper relationship building confrontation predicates itself on your psychological and behavioral personality styles. The more sincere and tactful you are, the better the chances are for a positive outcome. Yes indeed, "personalize!"

By personalizing how you apply the Confrontation Model's techniques, the more you present your true self. This helps to reduce any coldness or barrenness associated with the Confrontation Model. As you learn and feel more comfortable and confident with the Confrontation Model, you'll find yourself invoking the techniques without anyone ever realizing that you are using a strategic confrontation method. You will learn that as your confidence increases, personalizing becomes automatic! Confronting becomes easier, less stressful, and quite efficient. You will be able to confront simple to complex issues more often—undetected—and with more success.

There are two primary techniques which most learners want to personalize: the 1–2–3 Approach and asking for commitment. Most other aspects of the Confrontation Model will eventually and naturally become personalized but the two techniques mentioned will require your diligence and extensive use of your intent to personalize them.

Let's work on personalizing the 1–2–3 Approach first. Most learners have no problem personalizing the Intro. But let me remind you that it's your intent to reach

Win-Win-Win outcome. Many users want to personalize the techniques solely because they are afraid and want to mitigate rejection. That's the wrong reason for personalizing. Imagine yourself personalizing your fear of confronting—what a label to have embedded on your forehead for all to see. Instead, personalize your desire to easily initiate a confrontation which hopefully will seek a win-win-win collaboration.

Beginners may have trouble initially personalizing the C.C.S. They feel that if the recommended technique of stating the C.C.S. with a single word is too harsh. Personalizing this technique should reflect the "real you" and your cultural expressions or mannerisms; sometimes it can be done by voice inflection and nonverbals, or even a moment of silence. Suppose you are a parent and your daughter doesn't want to communicate with you because of a hurt feeling.

After your Intro, the C.C.S. can be presented as follows:

"Yes, I too, have trouble communicating.

Here we used six words as follows:

"Yes" :   emphasizes sincerity
"I, too":   stresses a sense of ownership and wisdom
"have trouble communicating":   underlines the *issue* and creates a bond between the owners of a similar *issue*. The CCS modifies the bombardment yet delivers the message behind the *issue*.

However, the focus now moves on to the FIX, which puts the creative solving activities in motion. Using the previous CCS, we need to set accountability constructively with the personal touch. We might try this statement:

"I need to know how we can improve the way we communicate with each other."

This statement continues to keep things personalized provided that the confronter maintains sincerity. The statement uses a "we" word rather than the "you" word. Yet it does not relinquish the confrontee's accountability to create a solution.

Putting this example into motion with harmony and sincerity are but two ways to personalize The 1–2–3 Approach. Getting rid of the "dumping on the confrontee" attitude is the basic ingredient for personalizing. Personalizing is word flow without intimidation and reflecting the authenticity of the confronter's intent. It's avoiding using "you" words as much as possible without the fear of transferring accountability for resolution onto the confrontee.

People who want to personalize a confrontion need to bear in mind that over-personalizing can become a disservice to both parties. It is important to be authentic and sincere as it is to be concise, tactful, and focused on restoring the *issue*. This brings us to the next plateau—asking for commitment.

Personalizing commitment needs to be constructed with motivating resolution in mind. By properly implementing commitment, we are arguing a planned outcome—a behavioral change in most cases. Obtaining proper commitment can be approached in many ways by the confronter. Personalizing commitment is highly recommended and encouraged. But do not personalize asking for commitment to the point that the confrontee realizes that you are not serious or are begging—that would be devastating.

Depending on your personality and mannerisms, approach the confrontee with a positive orientation as best as possible. Your words need not be threatening or demanding, but rather need to be firm indicating the seriousness of the commitment follow through. Asking for commitment several times in succession is an excellent method of demonstrating your firmness and your commitment to the confrontee's commitment.

Be creative when personalizing commitment. It's wide open from being direct with few words to that of being repetitive and even humorous. Always be yourself! Avoid being creative to the point where you are acting out what the confrontee wants to see and hear. It's always important to know that you are expressing your true self.

Conclusion

Centuries ago, the Samurai warrior went to battle. He took with him the Bushido philosophy, his skills, his confidence, his integrity, and his desire. He achieved great powers of concentration and awareness through constant practice.

The Samurai's visions went beyond the battle scene — the celebration of victory offered greater pride and value. Fear was not part of his armament. He created and lived his future, daily. Today, we can live in more peaceful surroundings. Only one enemy hides within us—FEAR—and its days are numbered!

Knowledge combats fear;
Confidence rids us of fear; and
Desire suffocates fear.

As a parent, spouse, manager, supervisor, teacher, nurse, professional, teenager, or whomever, *see a brighter future*. Desire that which is part of you in the future. Embrace it with love and make it so.

- Be a better listener
- Be a better confronter
- Be a better communicator
- Be happier at home and on the job
- Be more productive and be recognized for it
- Be confident, peaceful, and free

Finally, I have one last gift for you:

Remember, you are more than you know!

APPENDIX

Instructions for the Exercises

The self-learning exercises provide the reader with real-life scenarios most of which were contributed by *managers, supervisors, parents and professionals* over the past six years. The scenarios are of four levels of difficulty:

- ◆ Warm-ups
- ◆ Easy
- ◆ Moderate
- ◆ Difficult

Strategy Outlines for two or three scenarios for each category are presented for review. The outlines suggest a possible confrontation dialogue. These are not cast in stone, but serve as examples. You may find other dialogue more suitable for the same scenario. Use whatever works for you.

First, become familiar with the Confrontation Model and work through scenarios until you are confident that you could execute them. Each scenario contains:

- • Issue statement
- • Information about the situation
- • Descriptive information related to the characters involved. (Note: Warm-up scenarios omit descriptions.)

The self-paced developmental learning exercises are designed to provide structure and guidance into use of the Confrontation Model, particularly the *1–2–3 Approach, Facts, Win-Win-Win, Resolution,* and *Desired Outcome* as described in Chapter 5.

Instructions:

1. Read the scenario carefully and try to visualize it thoroughly
2. Use the empty lined space to replicate facts which pertain to the scenario. A brief explanation of confrontation scenario including: who's involved, complications, personal conflicts, problems, situational outcomes, and potential concerns.
3. Fill in the answers to each outline requirement
4. Some outline requirements require the stretching of your imagination; that is, you need to create a few facts related to the situation. You are also asked to perceive the situation through the *confrontee's* perspective.

5. Do your best to be as accurate as possible. *The Issue, The 1–2–3 Approach, the Win-Win-Win, Resolution or Desired Outcome* require utmost care when determining conclusions

6. Facts and rebuttals may seem arbitrary, i.e., not clear or focused. Remember, interpretations and perspectives of each scenario vary from person to person

7. It is recommended that a friend or peer provide you with input on how he interpreted the scenario. This feedback may be helpful to you.

Use a blank **Strategy Outline Guide Sheet** to help you prepare for each scenario. The outline provides guidance on how to develop, gather, and interpret information pertinent to each scenario. It offers the confronter an opportunity to sharpen his or her skills when investigating and presenting the facts related to the confrontation. You can also use the Guide Sheet for your practice confrontations.

(You have copyright permission to copy this outline for *personal use only*. Any other use violates copyright law.) Complete one Strategy Outline Sheet for each scenario.

A *sample* outline follows on the next page.

The Strategy Outline Guide Sheet

Scenario #:_____   Date:___ /___ /___
(For instructions, refer to the section on Strategy Outline presented earlier in Appendix A)

Brief explanation of confrontation scenario including: _____

_____

_____

_____

_____

* who's involved _____

* complications _____

* personal conflicts _____

* problems_____

* situational outcome _____

* potential concerns _____

* location or setting_____

1. The Issue: _____

2. The overall Desired Outcome (Resolution): _____

_____

_____

3. Possible interpretation of the Confrontee's perspective: _____

_____

_____

4. (THE 1–2–3 Approach):

• The Intro: _____

• The C.C.S.: _____

(Remember, The C.C.S. is eight words or less.)

• The Fix: _____

5. Fact #1: _____

6. Fact #2: _____

7. Fact #3: _____

8. Fact #4: _____

9. Acceptable Win-Win-Win: _____

10. Commitment Sought: _____

11. Your Follow-up to Confrontee's Commitment: _____

_____

_____

12. Your Follow-up to Your Commitment: _____

_____

_____

13. How will you ascertain (measure) the success of the Resolution, i.e., what constitutes the Resolve? _____

_____

14. Personal comments about the Issue and the Results of the confrontation: _____

_____

_____

_____

_____

NOTES

Did the confrontation succeed in accomplishing its desired outcome?

❐ Yes   ❐ No

What were your strong points _____

_____

What would you do differently? _____

General Notes: _____

_____

_____

_____

_____

_____

Individual Performance

The next important item is **FEEDBACK!!!** How well are we doing? And, what skills do we need to improve? The answers come from two sources:

1. *Your honest self-critique*
2. *Feedback from others.*

Feedback from friends and peers on your confrontation practice exercises provides you with valuable information. Use the **Individual Performance Critique Sheet** on the next page for your personal or peer evaluation.

(Permission is granted to copy the *Individual Performance Critique Sheet* for personal use only; any other use violates copyright laws.)

INDIVIDUAL PERFORMANCE CRITIQUE SHEET

Name _____.   Date: ___ / ___ / ___

Scenario_____ Evaluator _____

Categories for Evaluation	Needs Work	Okay	Very Good
1. Set the intention to Confront			
2. Self-confronted first			
3. Generated Attention			
4. Used Pre-Introduction intro			
5. Stated the C.C.S. properly			
6. Used the FIX properly			
7. Clearly presented the issue			
8. Stayed foced			
9. Remained emotionally clear			
10. Showed ability to communicate facts			
11. Offered the opportunity for collaboration			
12. Properly coached the confrontee			
13. Used the"Repeat the Fix" & Repaet C.C.S.			
14. Reached a Win-Win-Win outcome			
15. Had good control of time			
16. Stayed in control of the issue			
17. Got commitment			
18. Adhered to the Model guidelines			
19. Used empathy			
20. Demonstrated good nonverbal skills			
21. Showed consistency and leadership			
22. Provided good potential for resolution			

Warm-up Confrontation Scenarios

SCENARIO #1: *Teenager not doing his or her chore(s)*

1. **The Issue:** Jan, my daughter, didn't do the dishes last night. She had agreed to wash them after dinner, except on weekends.
2. **Desired Outcome:** To get Jan to keep her commitment to wash the dishes.
3. **Possible interpretation of the Confrontee's perspective:** She might have forgotten or was suddenly interrupted.
4. *THE 1–2–3 Approach:*
   The Intro: "Hi Jan, I would like to talk about a little issue. Is now okay?"
   The C.C.S.: "Last night's dishes were not done."
   The Fix: "What shall we do?"
5. **Rebuttal #1:** "I'm sorry. I forgot." (Note: this could be an outright lie.)
6. **Fact #1:** "I did them."
7. **Rebuttal #2:** "It won't happen again."
8. **Fact #2:** "You owe me one."
9. **Rebuttal #3:** "I said, I was sorry." (If necessary, repeat the Fix: "Then what shall we do about it?"
10. **Acceptable Win-Win-Win:** Jan must make up for last night and reaffirm her commitment to honor her agreement. In return, I will do my best to be patient with her and acknowledge that we all forget, once in a while.
11. **Commitment Sought:** A strong affirmation and a contingency plan should it happen again.
12. **Resolution:** I will show Jan my appreciation for her chores after each dish washing.

Personal Notes: This was a four-week agreement. I must interact with Jan as soon as possible after she has completed her chores.

SCENARIO #2: Employee (Joe) Is Taking Long Breaks.

1. **The Issue:** Taking long breaks.
2. **Desired Outcome:** Confrontee observes the allotted time for breaks.
3. **Possible confrontee's perspective:** "Everybody's taking long breaks, too! Why pick on me?"
4. *THE 1–2–3 Approach::*
   The Intro: "Hi, Joe. There's an issue we need to discuss."
   The C.C.S. "Taking long breaks."
   The Fix: "What are you going to do about it?"
5. **Rebuttal #1:** "It's not just me."
6. **Fact #1:** "True."
7. **Rebuttal #2:** "I'm not abusing the break periods."
8. **Fact #2:** "During the last two weeks, you have taken five extended breaks." (If necessary, repeat the Fix: "Joe, what are you going to do about it?")
9. **Acceptable Win-Win-Win:** Joe acknowledges his consistent long breaks, and he shows desire to correct the problem.
10. **Commitment Sought:** Joe promises not to take long breaks for the next 2 months.
11. **Resolution:** Your Follow-up to Confrontee's Commitment: At the end of the two months period, you will sit down with Joe and discuss his improvement. Or, if he does not succeed, you will immediately confront him, and discuss the new issue (possibly suspension).

Personal Notes: Each week, for the next two months, I will reinforce Joe's ability to take shorter breaks and keep his commitment.

Easy Confrontation Scenarios

SCENARIO #100: Spouse lied about whereabouts.

1. **The Issue:** Lying about whereabouts, which is unacceptable in a marital relationship.
2. **Desired Outcome:** Stop lying,–permanently!
3. **Possible confrontee's perspective:** It was just a little white lie. No big deal.
4. *THE 1–2–3 Approach:*
    The Intro: "John, I need to discuss a very important issue with you. Can we do it now?" (Wait for spouse's response: if yes, continue with the C.C.S.; if No, arrange a new time within an hour or so.)
    The C.C.S.: "Lying – I cannot tolerate that again."
    The Fix: "What are you going to do to prevent this from happening again?"
5. **Rebuttal #1:** "I wasn't really lying. Why are you getting so up-tight about it for?"
6. **Fact #1:** "You told me that you had to work late, but when I called back, I was informed that you actually left early with a friend."
7. Rebuttal #2: "I had to buy something at the store before it closed; something special for you."
8. **Fact #2:** "You came home two hours late and without anything for me."
9. **Rebuttal #3:** "It's a surprise!"
10. **Fact #3:** "Surprise or not … (repeat the Fix) … "What are you going to do to prevent lying to me again?"
11. **Acceptable Win-Win-Win:** There's only one solution for lying, i.e., no repeats. And that goes for both spouses.
12. **Commitment Sought:** Both spouses must demonstrate openness and honest exchanges. Agreement must be made to support this endeavor.
13. **Your Follow-up to Confrontee's Commitment:** Each week have an informal discussion on how much progress has been made in the areas of openness and honesty.

Personal Notes: Express my need to my spouse that I can not tolerate any form of lying, whatsoever. And further express my enjoyment that we can work it out.

SCENARIO #101: A Staff Member (Jim) Shows Up Unprepared For An Important Meeting.

1.   **The Issue:** Being unprepared.
2.   **Desired Outcome:** Jim is expected to have prepared a presentation for an important meeting.
3.   **Possible Confrontee's perspective:** He didn't have sufficient time and resources to prepare for the meeting.
4.   *THE 1–2–3 Approach:*
     The Intro: "Jim, we need to talk for a few minutes." (Wait for Jim's response.)
     The C.C.S.: "Your presentation; what happened?"
     The Fix: "What will you do to resolve this?"
5.   **Rebuttal #1:** "I didn't get the time to properly prep for the meeting. As a matter of fact, Mary Delaney never gave me the client charts. If she did her job, then I would have had all the information at the damn meeting!"
6.   **Fact #1:** "Jim, the issue is … you're being unprepared … recall, at our last staff meeting, you were also unprepared."
7.   **Rebuttal #2:** "There's just not enough time in the day to get all the information needed for these meetings."
8.   **Fact #2:** "Your function at these meetings is very important. Not having appropriate input is unacceptable."
9.   **Rebuttal #3:** "All these meetings get in the way of productivitity."
10. **Fact #3:** Meetings are important to company communication…repeat the Fix … What are you going to do?"
11. **Acceptable Win-Win-Win:** Jim must take responsibility for being prepared at his meetings, and to let me know immediately if he anticipates any hindrances to accomplishing this.
12. **Commitment Sought:** Jim must express that he is accountable and understands the importance of being prepared for future meetings.
13. **Your Follow-up to Confrontee's Commitment:** Since Jim is a good worker, I will briefly critique his performance after each meeting for some period of time.

Personal Notes: I will also do my part to evaluate the effectiveness of these meetings with the other members involved.

SCENARIO #102: Teenage daughter has been hanging around questionable friends. Lately, your teenage child's attitude and language has become negative and disrespectful. She has openly informed you that her new crowd as influenced her. You've spoken about this situation before, and she consented that everything was cool and "Don't worry." But this is no longer true.

1. **The Issue:** She came home late last night and smelt of cigarette smoke

2. **Desired Outcome:** Have your daughter break away from the crowd and learn from the experience.

3. **Possible *confrontee's* perspective:** Everything is still "cool." You're just overly concerned and too protective.

4. *THE 1–2–3 Approach*
   The Intro: "Hi, Jeanne! Can we chat for a couple of minutes?" (Wait for daughter's response.)
   The *C.C.S.* "The crowd's negative influence on you."
   The Fix: "What can *we* do about it?"

5. *Rebuttal #1:* "Oh! That again"

6. *Fact #1:* "Last night, you came home after midnight.

7. *Rebuttal #2:* "You're always on my case."

8. *Fact #2:* "We've discussed this before, Jeanne. I'm willing to assist, but what can you do about it?"

9. **Rebuttal #3:** "I'm confused. Sometimes I feel great when I'm with them, and sometimes I feel used by them."

10. **Fact #3:** "It seems to me that you are being used more than you admit to yourself."

11. **Acceptable *Win-Win-Win:*** If Jeanne recommends a viable solution on breaking away from the negative crowd, I (the parent) will assist and support her in the process.

12. **Commitment Sought:** She realizes that the crowd is, indeed, negatively influencing her. And that she convinces me of that.

13. **Your Follow-up to Confrontee's Commitment:** Work daily and consistently with Jeanne to re-affirm her commitment and support her efforts.

Personal Notes: Become more aware of my children's friends on a personal basis.

Moderate Confrontation Scenarios

SCENARIO #200: My husband has gained about 10 pounds. Most of this is due to too many beers and a lot of unnecessary snacks. He feel that it's okay and appropriate for his age. The situation is complicated, though, by his obnoxious demeanor after drinking.

1.   **The Issue:** Obnoxious demeanor towards his wife.
2.   Desired Outcome: Regain respect and demeanor and reduce the drinking.
3.   **Possible confrontee's perspective:** Wife is getting touchy and can't handle the little fun and release of tension that he is having, once in a while.
4.   *THE 1–2–3 Approach:*
    The Intro: "Jack, we need to discuss an issue. Can we do it now, before dinner?" (Wait for husband's response.)
    THE C.C.S.: "Our relationship lacks the respect I need."
    The Fix: "What can we do to change that?"
5.   **Rebuttal #1:** "What are you talking about?"
6.   **Fact #1:** "After you drink a few beers, you tend to talk down to me."
7.   **Rebuttal #2:** "It's your imagination!"
8.   **Fact #2:** "Last night you called me a dumb broad. I didn't appreciate those words."
9.   Rebuttal #3: "Ha! Now you're getting sensitive."
10.   **Fact #3:** "Then you told me that I didn't look sexy enough for you. That really hurt me."
11.   **Rebuttal #4:** "Well, I had a few beers. I didn't mean it that way."
12.   **Fact #4:** (repeat the Fix) "What can you do to change this?"
13.   **Acceptable Win-Win-Win:** Jack needs to show more respect to his wife and slow down on the beers. The wife will take the necessary steps to distract Jack from the beers and snacks.
14.   **Commitment Sought:** Make a firm decision to cut down on the food and beer intake and be more sensitive to his wife.
15.   **Your Follow-up to c onfrontee's Commitment:** Give him feedback each night about his progress and how better you feel because of his concern for you.

Personal Notes: Don't let little annoyances go on past the point that you recognized their existence.

SCENARIO #201: You are doing your compliance inspection in the production area. You observe an operator's assistant taking his time (pacing) and allowing a build up of cases. His slow performance needs to be addressed. As you approach him, he says: "I'm tired of this job. I want to be an operator."

1. **The Issue:**   Poor performance
2. **Desired Outcome:**   (1) to resolve the issue of pacing; (2) to evaluate the request for a promotion.
3. **Possible confrontee's perspective:** He could be interested in a better and more responsible position. However, at this time, it looks like the he's trying to Overshoot with fast defensive statements (a defense mechanism) to cover up his poor performance.
4. *THE 1–2–3 Approach:*
    The Intro: "Well, let's talk about it; OK?"
    THE C.C.S.:   "First of all, let's discuss the pacing."
    The Fix: "How do you propose improving your pace?"
5. **Rebuttal #1:**   "It's the job; I'm bored."
6. **Fact #1:**   "Pacing doesn't get you promoted."
7. **Rebuttal #2:** "You don't have plans to promote me."
8. **Fact #2:**   "You haven't hinted or requested a promotion before, but I'll work on it with you."
9. **Acceptable Win-Win-Win:**   (Employee) Improve performance immediately. (Supervisor) Evaluate opportunities for worker's promotion.
10. **Commitment Sought:**   For the employee to demonstrate required level of performance.
11. **Your Follow-up to Confrontee's Commitment:** To stop by periodically and reinforce relationship. Also, to further discuss employee's interest and potential opportunities for promotion.

Personal Notes: Don't take for granted that workers are contented about their job. Develop a program for reviewing job expectations, career potentials, and opportunities.

SCENARIO #202: You suspect your teenage son, Richard, to be smoking marijuana. Several times you have noticed him acting silly and starry-eyed. Lately, he's been up in his room more than usual and even his friend Jimmy has been acting odd when the boys are together.

1. **The Issue:** Richard may be smoking pot and that is not allowed.
2. Desired Outcome: You want to know if the boys are smoking pot; and if so, to stop using it.
3. **Possible confrontee's perspective:** Getting a little high is nothing to worry about.
4. *THE 1–2–3 Approach:*
    The Intro: "Richard, I have a concern I need to talk to you about. OK?"
    THE C.C.S.: "Smoking pot."
    The Fix: "What are you going to do about it?"
5. **Rebuttal #1:** "Who me?"
6. **Fact #1:** "I can smell it in your room."
7. **Rebuttal #2:** "What are you trying to tell me, mom?"
8. **Fact #2:** "Smoking pot is not allowed – in your room or elsewhere!"
9. **Rebuttal #3:** "And?"
10. **Fact #3:** (Repeat the Fix) "Richard, I want to work this out with you. What are you going to do about it?"
11. **Acceptable WIN-WIN-Win:** Richard admits his usage and is willing to discuss the issue further.
12. **Commitment Sought:** (1) his openness and honesty towards you; (2) Richard will stop smoking pot, (3) he will discuss the matter with Jimmy.
13. **Your Follow-up to Confrontee's Commitment:** Have Jimmy and Richard affirm their commitment to you when asked.

Personal Notes: Richard is best approached with respect. This avoids prompting his defensive reactions.

Difficult Confrontation Scenarios

SCENARIO #300: One of your top performing employees (Geoffry) has a serious HYGIENE problem. As a matter of fact, it is a putrefaction (a foul-smelling body odor). Several of his work cohorts have consistently complained, but you were too embarrassed to deal with the person. Now, to make things worse, two employees have put in for a transfer. How can you resolve this?

1. **The Issue:** Eliminating the body odor.
2. **Desired Outcome:** Geoffry becomes aware of and resolves the social dilemma.
3. **Possible interpretation of the confrontee's perspective:** Geoffry does not realize that his odor is disrupting to others.
4. *THE 1–2–3 Approach:*
   The Intro: "Hi there, Geoffry! Would you please see me in my office for a few minutes before the end of the day. I need to ask you a favor. OK?"
   THE C.C.S.: "Geoffry … pause … you have a severe case of body odor."
   The Fix: "How do you propose to handle the condition?"
5. **Rebuttal #1:** "My wife likes it. I see no problem."
6. **Fact #1:** "The odor is disturbing to me and others in our area."
7. **Rebuttal #2:** "There are things that I don't like about them, too."
8. **Fact #2:** "It is a health and social problem which needs to be resolved."
9. **Rebuttal #3:** "Buy an air refresher for the area."
10. **Fact #3:** "What are you going to do about it?"
11. **Rebuttal #4:** "I don't feel I have a problem."
12. **Fact #4:** "What are you going to do about it?"
13. **Silence …**
14. **Rebuttal #5:** "I'll see a doctor."
15. **Fact #5:** "Good. I'll work with you on this. It's a difficult situation."
16. **Acceptable Win-Win-Win:** Geoffry recognizes and takes corrective action to resolve the situation. As for your part, you will inform the other workers and ask for their patience and cooperation.
17. **Commitment Sought:** Continued improvement.
18. **Your Follow-up to Confrontee's Commitment:** Will have more frequent visits with Geoffry and inform him of his progress.

Personal Notes: Never let this kind of condition go unattended. It gets worse by the day: emotionally, socially, and otherwise.

SCENARIO #301 My spouse has been eating a lot and gaining weight. We have had minor discussions about this situation before. He/she has put on at least 35 pounds and feels very uncomfortable and frustrated. A new problem as occurred as well. Now our sexual life is going sour because my spouse is embarrassed and doesn't feel sexually attractive.

Despite the poor eating habits, you have observed that your spouse's self-esteem and confidence has been weakening and suffering substantial lose. What issue(s) are you going to confront?

1. **The Issue(s):** Excessive eating has caused a weight increase, however, the implication of low self-esteem exists. The symptom is being overweight. The cause may be something else (unknown). Other symptoms are diminishing confidence and low sexual appeal.
   A viable issue is to communicate the need for improve self-esteem.
2. **Desired Outcome:** To get my spouse to open up and confront himself/herself.
3. **Possible confrontee's perspective:** The world caving in on me. It's hopeless. Or, it's all your fault!
4. *THE 1–2–3 Approach:*
   The Intro: "Sweetheart, I think you and I need to talk about a few things. Is now a good time to chat?" (If "No", then ask for a specific time and get commitment on it, too.)
   THE C.C.S.: "I sense the need to improve your self-esteem."
   The Fix: "Can we work on improving your self-esteem, together?"
5. **Rebuttal #1:** "I don't know what to say. I just don't feel like doing anything."
6. **Fact #1:** "It's obvious that your health needs attention."
7. **Rebuttal #2:** "That can change. What's a few pounds?"
8. **Fact #2:** "Our sex life has just about stopped!"
9. **Rebuttal #3:** "So? There are many reasons for that."
10. **Fact #3:** "Sweetheart, I am willing to work and support you. But I need to know what you are going to do about improving your self-esteem?"
11. **Acceptable Win-Win-Win:** Spouse agrees to focus on improving self-esteem. And you agree to encourage him/her in the process.
12. Commitment Sought: A firm decision and a kiss, etc.
13. **Your Follow-up to Confrontee's Commitment:** Ask occasionally for insight on spouse's progress.

Personal Notes: Never let things get this far along before confronting them.

The Rules

1: When you truly understand what others are saying, then and only then, can you correctly respond.

2: Underlying almost every confrontation problem is a communication problem.

3: The best preventive medicine for problems is accurate communication—confronting the issue at hand.

4: Express what you feel – that's your only obligation. Be truthful about it! That's the breath of life. There's no hidden intention, motive or agenda. It's a feeling of *freedom*, it instills *confidence*. It earns *respect*. It's *fun*. It really is!

5: The success of the initial communication is solely the responsibility of the sender.

6: During the initial communication, the sender must demand full attention from the receiver. If not, then the receiver is not fully attentive. Do not proceed – stop! Repeat from the beginning if appropriate.

7: The Receiver is responsible for giving the sender a *convincing acknowledgment*.

8: Take communication seriously. True Understanding is an end product, i.e., a commodity, with a price tag, and becomes a corporate or personal asset. Constantly strive for excellent communications within our companies, families, and relationships.

9: Each cycle is complete. The conversation does not need to progress. The bottom line – IF True Understanding is still required, then and only then need you proceed.

10: Try to get a True Understanding in each Cycle of Communication – make every effort to do so.

11: It is best not to proceed with the conversation until both Sender and Receiver know exactly what is being communicated.

12:     When we abstain from pre-judging the outcome, positively or negatively, we sharpen our ability to clearly present the facts and relate them to the issue.

13:     Keep the Issue separate from the Confrontee as much as possible, especially at the onset of the confrontation.

14:     "You" and "they" are confronting the Issue, not confronting each other.

15:     Don't personalize the Issue or the confrontation.

16:     Do not proceed beyond the Intro unless you get 100% attention from the confrontee(s).

17:     Use eight (8) words or less for the C.C.S.

18:     Your fundamental concern in the Fix is to protect the *transfer of accountability* and *return* proper resolution of the *issue* to the Confrontee.

19:     "The Shorter the Better."

20:     Simply state only *one* fact to support your position on the issue. *Do not rattle-off* a series of facts.

21:     Repeat the Fix when the confrontee tries to escape accountability for the issue yet has already admitted or acknowledged ownership for resolving the issue. The confrontee attempts to manipulate facts or control the dialogue.

22:     Repeat the C.C.S. whenever the confronter (you) or the confrontee losses focus of the issue. Repeating the C.C.S. invariably brings the issue back in focus.

23:     Never back down. Always proceed. If troubled, Repeat the Fix or the C.C.S. That will give you time, and make the confrontee realize that you are serious.

24:     You do not have to respond to anything except the facts. If it is not factual, then proceed to your next fact (Facts #2 and #3) or repeat the Fix or C.C.S.

25:     Keep your facts up to date and well documented when discussing ongoing matters. Do not go into shock. State a supportive fact as to the time, place, and date. And repeat the Fix or C.C.S.

26:     Avoid shouting or screaming at a passive confrontee as an attempt to stimulate him (shouting is never recommended). Talk slowly, very clearly, and ask for a response. Use questions and ask for facts. Be polite and respectful.

27:     Don't necessarily disagree with the rationalization or intellectualization. If they are true, then there's no reason for the Confrontee to further their escape. Stay focused on the issue. Repeat the Fix or the C.C.S. — that's the real and current Issue.

28:     Avoid all unnecessary conversations once on the pyramid.

29:     Always look directly into the face of the Confronter. Never look away.

30:     When the Emergency Stop is invoked, always set a new time, date, and place to continue the confrontation.

31:     Never apologize.

32:     Return and continue the confrontation within 24 hours.

33:     Always remain silent after you present your facts, especially when you are near the top of the pyramid. After 15 seconds of dead silence, repeat the Fix or the C.C.S.

34:     The Confronter's intention must be to reach a Win–Win–Win outcome.

35:     The more sincere the Intent, the stronger the subliminal message of your sincerity will be. This encourages the confrontee to seek a Win–Win–Win Resolution.

36:     The confronter must sense the Confrontee's Commitment. The confrontee must express it in a manner that shows it comes from the heart.

37:     The Confrontation dialogue (i.e., the Confrontation Model process) is not complete until Resolution is acknowledged by the confronter.

38: Separate from the *Confrontee* immediately after the Commitment. It is better not to discuss the Confrontation with the **Confrontee**. *At that* time, you are presenting a personal empowerment skill. You are showing decision-making and leadership abilities. Do not dilute it by rehashing it with the confrontee.

39: The person who confronts must concentrate on the Issue at all times.

40: Do not proceed with the confrontation until you have clarified the Issue.

41: Avoid prejudging. Don't react in haste. Don't assume your interpretation of nonverbals is always 100% accurate.

42: *Ask probing questions to clarify your interpretations. Act calmly and sincerely. Instill confidence in the confrontee that you understand his or her situation.*

43: Make every effort to stand when confronting. Try to stand between 3 and 5 feet apart.

44: Given multiple issues, confront the most important *issue* first.

45: Separate each *issue* and give each *issue* its own pyramid.

46: Seek a Win-Win-Win orientation. The closer you get to the truth of any *issue*, the greater the Commitment — the greater the Resolve!

47: Always attempt to collaborate upwards on the pyramid. Ask for the facts. Encourage the confrontee to contribute to the Win-Win-Win situation.

48: The moment someone confronts you (spontaneously), you become the receiver of the conversation — the confrontee.

49: If caught in a spontaneous confrontation; you must become the Sender — the Confronter—as quickly as possible.

50: Your Intent: Find out the *issue*.

51: Avoid spontaneous confrontations with hostiles. Set the confrontation up carefully.

52: Never get emotional with hostiles.

53:     Be concise and precise: always factual.

54:     Never get off on tangents — stay on the issue.

55:     Talk slowly, firmly, clearly, and with confidence!

56:     Repeat the 1–2–3 Approach, i.e., the C.C.S. or the FIX, as often as necessary.

57:     Do not ever speak immediately after *YOU* asked a question or demanded an answer. Stay totally silent, even for a minute, if necessary.

58:     Always look at the "snip" face-to-face, and if necessary, eye-to-eye.

59:     Invoke the Emergency Stop if he or she gets out of hand; but never permit the confrontation to go permanently unresolved.

On-the-Floor-Coaching

"Where the rubber meets the road."

So what is *On-The-Floor-Coaching?* Succinctly, one-to-one coaching between the trainer (coach, facilitator or consultant) and the manager or supervisor. OTFC is the action taken by the trainer who rolls up his sleeves, goes out to the work area (plant, office, field) and performs one-to-one job related training with the manager or supervisor.

OTFC is the substance behind *thorough* supervisory training:

- It is the *force* which drives managers and supervisors to proper behavioral change.
- It is the *trust* that converts knowledge into action.
- Without OTFC, training labs tend to regress to seminars which rarely lead to any long-term change.

OTFC is the *reinforcement process* reiterating topics presented in the training labs. As the OTFC relationship matures, advanced and more personal exchanges of information occur. In many cases, it is through the *techniques* of professional consulting that supervisors learn how to perform the job with more sophistication:

- Better communications
- Proficient confrontations
- Improved problem identification and solving
- Stronger team-building
- Keener sense of business and operations
- Provokes definite results-oriented thinking
- Saves time and money

OTFC is a science not widely practiced by trainers. One of the main reasons for that shortcoming is that many trainers truly do not have the experience beyond the "classroom or seminar" level. T*o be able to sit, stand, walk, and talk the same lan-*

guage of the supervisor or manager is not an easy task. It takes great skill, knowledge, and fortitude.

Two key critical situations where OTFC techniques are provided is presented below:

1. Confrontational Situations

The supervisor and OTFC Coach walk past several workstations, such as machine presses, assembly line, packaging areas, and typist's desk, and observe lower than normal performance by an operator. However, the supervisor continues walking without further investigating or confronting the poor performance.

The trainer-coach interjects, and asks the supervisor if he observed poor performance on the part of the operator. The supervisor's two possible replies follow:

a) If the supervisor said: "No," the OTFC trainer-coach focuses on developing the supervisor's awareness of the perception process, how to take better observations, identifying work and behavioral problems, some basic aspect and concepts of organizational behavior, production and productivity.

b) If the supervisor said "Yes," the OTFC trainer-coach focuses on any combination of the following: leadership skills, communication and confrontation skills, enforcing discipline, behavior, self-esteem, roles and purpose of supervision. Also, depending on the amount of OTFC already given to the supervisor, the trainer-coach might very well confront the supervisor and demand better performance.

In either case, the OTFC trainer-coach is ready to instruct, lead, and provide managerial role-model-like behavior. It is a Win-Win-Win situation.

2. Situations During Meetings

For this example, we assume that the OTFC trainer-coach and the manager have been working on an OTFC relationship for at least three weeks. During a regularly held weekly meeting, the trainer-coach observes that his client, the manager, does not perform effectively in meetings. The coach also observes that the meeting itself needs improvement. The OTFC trainer-coach realizes that the manager portrays a passive role and does not support the demands obligated during the meeting. Conversation not only lacks factual data, it also does not focus on clarifying issues or attaining results. The absence of results-oriented thinking and accountability exists.

The OTFC trainer-coach has several options:

- Interject and serve as a coach to all members of the group
- Confer with the manager after the meeting and discuss the particulars observed

- Based on agreement with the manager, intercede on behalf of the manager and conduct the meeting exemplifying role-model-like manager behavior.

(Note: Avoid telling your client how to run his business. Your role and purpose is to demonstrate how to improve the conducting of meetings.)

As you can see from these two examples, OTFC demands expertise and a trainer-coach with strong character. Numerous opportunities and situations exist whereby OTFC activities can foster substantial supervisory change. Realize the fact that *one-to-one reinforcement skills training* provides crucial input for managerial and supervisory development.

Corporate Application Guidelines

Reality vs. the Classroom

Training workshops or labs need not deal only in the theoretical. A good lab turns theory into practical knowledge for real life and work applications. It further solicits the managers and supervisors to bring situational examples from the job and brings them into the lab.

The lab is an experimental arena where the supervisors, as participants, learn by practice and trial and error involvements. This setting reduces most personal intimidations from any wrong doing or slow learning. In the lab setting, "right or wrong" is not considered. Instead, the lab is a place where "what is best" gets reinforced. It is a place where supervisors and managers can "bring it to the lab," so to speak. Some of the most stubborn and closed-minded supervisors have evolved from these labs to become staunch supporters.

Senior Management Support

The overall application of Confrontation Training within any organization requires an interactive format. The decision making body, the CEO and Senior Management personnel, must agree upon certain rules and conditions.

The following ten *application guidelines* provide information regarding the installation of Confrontation training in the corporate setting:

1. **There must be top-down management support and commitment.** Commitment is not to be in the form of a single memo or statement from the executive. It must be continuous. A good chance exists that the supervisor or manager, over the years, has lost faith in the management. Hence, they no longer see any personal benefit from change. The net result of that apathy is *resistance*, something very familiar to us.

2. **Listening:** Bottom-up communications eventually occur. Here, the key element by senior management is *listening*. This practice serves to convince supervisors of an important fact: "Yes, we (management) do listen and we do care."

3. **Visibility:** Senior management's frequent visits to the shop or mill area offers major impact. These areas include the manager and supervisor's

offices, the production area, and administrative offices. *Visibility* and interest in what the workers have to say about productivity is important. Just talking and socializing— "How are you doing today?"—provokes nonsense. Trivial talk is not substantial. Ask the operator of a machine what he or she recommends.

If you want to see an increase in loyalty and profits, then get out there and show them you care—that's motivation! When you are present in the production area with the hourly employees and show that they are respected for their work, you ensure recognition. Tell them how important their work is, the company's work is, and that we are all improving. These are some of the ways required for developing higher employee job satisfaction.

4. **Top-down training:** Before any of the mid-management, supervisory, or hourly training begins in the lab setting, senior management needs to get at least an overview. To obtain the best results and consistent support, we highly recommended that all senior management staff go through an abbreviated training program.

    One week after the senior management program began, the mid-manager's labs should start. This program should receive the full course agenda. Experience tells us that participants of this group work their way through the program at a quicker pace than the supervisory group.

    Then begin the supervisory group within one week of the managers' first lab. Probably prepare to extend the training labs an extra few weeks in order to accommodate different levels of education and learning abilities.

5. **Situational Scenarios:** On the job, real life situations can be collected from the training participants. Scenarios are easily requested as "homework" assignments between labs. In turn, they are used in the labs as application situations. Participants' skills can then get reinforced applied back on the job.

6. **Session Lengths**: Training labs for senior management should last at least one and a half hours (90 minutes). All other labs should last for three hours (it's a 24 hours program), with a five minute break in between. Try to keep the lab size limited to a maximum of 14 participants.

7. **Number of labs:** Hold at least two labs for senior management. The second could be in the form of an advance lab, after which the facilitator could offer some objective feedback. Please note: the facilitator of the senior management lab needs to demonstrate expertise in the field, and not succumb by intimidation from the group.

    Plan labs for mid-managers, supervisors, and selected employees on a weekly basis. A minimum of eight 3-hour labs are necessary. The Confrontation Skills Training Program uses a 24-hour design. Any combination is workable. Use of audio-visual equipment is essential.

    Basically, labs should last until you observe a desired behavioral change. Trainees need to demonstrate consistent application of the Confrontation Model skills. As a complementary program during and after the labs, perform *on-the-floor-coaching* as discussed in Appendix F.

8. **Evaluation**: Peers should critique each other. A major role developed in the labs for supervisors and managers is becoming a co-trainer. Peers need each other's support and prompt feedback; it also develops camaraderie. Overall, it helps build a strong team of managers and supervisors.

9. **Consistent Competencies:** Upon completion of the training programs, augment a three-month evaluation and follow-up program. Do this periodically, based on organizational needs and criteria based competencies requirements.

10. **Advanced Labs:** Advanced sessions can be held once the individuals have mastered the basics. Spontaneous confrontation activities and confrontation debates can further be explored and practiced. Once the participants demonstrate control and maturity, these labs serve as catalyst for vigorous problem solving endeavors.

The ten Application Guidelines presented inform the corporate trainer with a workable understanding of the Confrontation Model Training program. Details of the training contents and instructional guides have been partially presented within this book. However, based on the organization's needs and environment, customizing may prove necessary.

This book highlights many of the basic details of the Confrontation Model Training Program, as performed by the author and his staff. An experienced corporate trainer, with excellent confrontation skills and well versed in organizational and behavioral competencies, can install this program.

Should you require further assistance, the author's agency may be contacted for information from an advisory standpoint. Depending on need, full consultation and installation can be arranged (see Appendix "J" for details).

Lost Time Chart

If the value of efficient communication in the workplace is not truly understood, the Communication Lost Time Chart demonstrates the need and potential savings. The guidelines and chart below provide a simplified way of estimating a dollar value in savings generated by a company. Use the chart and modify it as to align to your company's situation. Remember, eliminating nonproductive chatter reduces the liability for lower profits. Socializing is an integrated aspect of the workplace and is okay, but frivolous chatter is pure loss.

1. The number of people working for your company = (A).

2. Estimated wasted people-seconds per employee per day = (B) {assume 180 seconds}

3. Multiply number of employees (A) by (B) wasted people-seconds per *employee* per day to get the number of wasted *people-seconds* per day company-wide (C) .

4. Divided wasted people-seconds per day (C) by 3600 sec/hr to get *wasted people-hours* per day (D)

5. Multiply (D) wasted hours per day by 250 work days per year to get *wasted people-hours per year.* (E)

6. Multiply your company's average hourly compensation rate (F) and the wasted people-hours per year (E) to get estimated cost of wasted time per year. This is the company's estimated annual savings.

Example:

1. Number of employees   300   (A)
2. Determine wasted people-seconds per employee per day   180   (B)
3. Calculate "wasted people–seconds" per day   Multiply (A x B)   54,000   (C)
4. Divide (C) by 3600 sec/hr to get "wasted people/hours per day   15   (D)
5. Multiply (D) by 250 workdays per year   3,750   (E)
6. Determine average employee compensation rate $12.00   (F)
7. Multiply (E x F) $45,000   (G)
8. "G" calculated is the estimated "wasted time per year

☛☛☛ *Your company's estimated annual savings $45,000*

1. Number of employees   _____ (A)
2. Determine wasted people-seconds per employee per day   _____ (B)
3. Calculate "wasted people–seconds" per day   Multiply (A x B)   _____ (C)
4. Divide (C) by 3600 sec/hr to get "wasted people/hours per day   _____ (D)
5. Multiply (D) by 250 workdays per year   _____ (E)
6. Determine average employee compensation rate   _____ (F)
7. Multiply (E x F)   _____ (G)
8. "G" calculated is the estimated "wasted time per year

☛☛☛ *Your company's estimated annual savings* $_____,_____.

Wallet size Reference Guide

Wallet size *Confrontation Model Reference Guides* are available. Carry one around with you or give them away as gifts. They are laminated and in color. Large quantity discounts available. Send $4.00 includes S&H, or send $3.00 with a SASE to Oughten House Foundation.

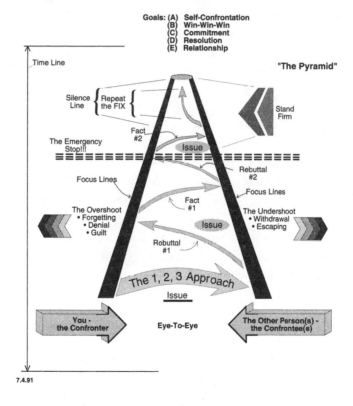

(Diagram not actual size)

About the Author

Robert Gerard began his working career as a civil engineer. Finding his interests lay with people, not things, he went back to college and completed a Bachelor's Degree in Social Psychology (1978) and a Master's Degree in Management and Organizational Psychology (1981). He has also completed the required course work for doctorates in Educational Management at Georgia State University and Spiritual Psychology at the California Institute for Integral Studies. In 1998, Robert earned his Ph.D. in Psychology of Spirituality at the College of Metaphysical Science.

He has worked as an Organizational Psychologist and Corporate Consultant specializing in improving communication and resolving conflicts within entire companies. The experiential methods he used for the creative handling of confrontations eventually found their way into written form in his book, *Handling Verbal Confrontation: Take the Fear Out of Facing Others.*

Robert's work experience spans over thirty-five years and crosses major industries: engineering, manufacturing, banking, education, and publishing. He has held consulting contracts for many major corporations, chaired an international convention, and spearheaded the start up efforts for the National Safety Council's "Safety Training Institute" for Western US and Pacific Rim regions.

Inspired by his inner guidance, Robert started Oughten House Publications in 1992. As visionary and President, Oughten House within six years has become a world leader in the metaphysical and Self-Mastery books. He then launched Oughten House Foundation, Inc., a worldwide educational and networking nonprofit organization advocating spiritual awakening, Self-Mastery, and DNA healing. His latest book, *DNA Healing Techniques: The How-To Handbook of DNA Expansion and Rejuvenation* was released.

Robert sustains a private counseling practice and continues to offer lectures, seminars, and workshops on: Confrontation Skills Training, Spirituality in the Workplace, Confronting Self-Truths, DNA Healing Techniques, and Self-Mastery. He offers assistance to people who wish to self-publish or co-publish their works. In addition to these books, Robert has also written two novels: *Lady from Atlantis* and *The Corporate Mule.*

Author-Reader Exchange Forum

Any inquiries, feedback, or comments that you would like to offer the author are welcomed. Please feel free to forward your thoughts to the address below.

An *Author-Reader Exchange Forum* has been developed. Questions on how to use the Communication and Confrontation Models will be acknowledged. Interactions among readers, trainers, and consultants of the Foundation's Faculty Group are encouraged. A *newsletter* will eventually evolve from these interactions.

Several editions of *Handling Verbal Confrontation* are planned, targeting certain industries (safety, construction, manufacturing, public service) or demographic populations (teenagers, marrieds, the elderly). The text and sample scenarios will be streamlined to meet the needs of that targeted group. Specialists in these various fields will co-author the text.

On-Site Training Programs are also available by Affiliate Members of the Foundation's Faculty Group throughout the nation.

Licensing Agreements for Instructors and Hosts are available for independent professionals who work directly with the public sectors in the fields of counseling, social service, parenting, and education. Please inquire about our licensing requirements and business arrangement.

For additional information, please write to:

OUGHTEN HOUSE FOUNDATION, INC.

P.O. Box 1059 • Coarsegold, California, 93614

Phone: (559) 641-7950 • Fax: (559) 641-7952

E-mail: HVC@oughtenhouse.com • Internet: www.oughtenhouse.com

Robert V. Gerard's personal E-mail: Robs1World@aol.com

Notes

Notes

Notes

Notes

Notes